TILING

Planning ▪ Layout ▪ Installation

FROM THE EDITORS OF **Fine Homebuilding**®

The Taunton Press

The Taunton Press, Inc., 63 South Main Street, PO Box 5506, Newtown, CT 06470-5506

e-mail: tp@taunton.com

Jacket/Cover Design: Cathy Cassidy

Interior Design: Cathy Cassidy

Layout: Cathy Cassidy

Front Cover Photographer: Charles Bickford, courtesy *Fine Homebuilding*, © The Taunton Press, Inc.

Back Cover Photographers: (clockwise from top left) Kevin Ireton, courtesy *Fine Homebuilding*, © The Taunton Press, Inc.; Charles Bickford, courtesy *Fine Homebuilding*, © The Taunton Press, Inc.; Charles Bickford, courtesy *Fine Homebuilding*, © The Taunton Press, Inc.; Roe A. Osborn, courtesy *Fine Homebuilding*, © The Taunton Press, Inc.

Taunton's For Pros By Pros® and Fine Homebuilding® are trademarks of The Taunton Press, Inc., registered in the U.S. Patent and Trademark Office.

Library of Congress Cataloging-in-Publication Data

Tiling : planning, layout, and installation.
   p. cm.
 "From the editors of Fine homebuilding."
 ISBN 1-56158-788-5
 1. Tile laying. I. Fine homebuilding.
 TH8531.T565 2005
 698--dc22

2005009162

Printed in the United States of America

10 9 8 7 6 5 4 3 2

The following manufacturers/names appearing in *Tiling* are trademarks:

Accuride®, Ben & Jerry's®, Blum®, Bosch®, Cheerios®, Chloraloy®, Dawn ®, Durock®, Enduro Poly™, Frisbee®, JDR Microdevices®, KV® 1385, MAPEI®, Minwax®, NuTone®, Panasonic®, Plexiglas®, Polyshades®, Rev-a-Shelf®, Stand Off®, Sub-Zero®, TiteBond®, Ultralume™, Waterlox®, Woodworker's Supply®

Special thanks to the authors, editors, art directors, copyeditors and other staff members of *Fine Homebuilding* who contributed to the development of the articles in this book.

CONTENTS

PART 3: AROUND THE HOUSE

INTRODUCTION

Fifty years ago, tile was the undisputed king in kitchens and baths. But today it's trumped by vinyl floors, laminate counters, and fiberglass tub surrounds whenever economy and convenience are paramount. Where quality and aesthetics rule, tile competes with hardwoods, granite, and solid-surface materials.

But in the end, tile is still king. No other material offers so many colors, sizes, shapes, and designs in a natural material that is so exceedingly beautiful. And centuries-old installations in Europe and Asia attest to the durability of tile. I seriously doubt that centuries from now tourists will flock to see a vinyl floor or fiberglass tub the way they flock to the Alhambra in Spain to marvel at the incredible mosaics.

In order to last, though, tile must be installed correctly, and that's where this book can help. Collected here are 18 articles from past issues of *Fine Homebuilding* magazine, written by professional tile setters, and describing the techniques that work for them.

You'll notice that most of the articles in this book are written by Tom Meehan, who along with his wife, Lane, runs Cape Cod Tileworks in Harwich, Massachusetts. Tom has been sharing his hard-won knowledge of tile setting with readers of *Fine Homebuilding* since 1991. A skilled craftsman and a generous teacher, Tom deserves the lion's share of the credit for making this book possible. If you buy this book, you'll be indebted to him, as am I and all the readers of *Fine Homebuilding*.

—Kevin Ireton, editor,
Fine Homebuilding

Upgrading to a Tile Shower

■ BY TOM MEEHAN

When fiberglass shower units were first introduced in the 1970s, they were the stars of the plumbing world. Inexpensive and relatively easy to install, they didn't crack and were easy to clean. Fiberglass units had their own problems, but they worked.

These days, bathrooms are a big renovation target for many homeowners, who might not know how to deal with their old fiberglass tub/shower units (see the photo at left). For this project, I removed the old tub unit in pieces, did a little carpentry and had the plumber relocate the drain and mixing valve for $400 or $500*. After that, the job was like any other: a site-built pan, backer board substrate and tile (in this case limestone) combined with some interesting details that made a luxurious shower (see the photo on the facing page).

Price estimates noted are from 2004.

Tom Meehan is a second-generation tile installer, owner of Cape Cod Tileworks in Harwich, Massachusetts, and co-author of Build Like a Pro® Working With Tile *(The Taunton Press, Inc., 2005).*

Demolition

The fun stage with quick results.

To take out the existing shower unit, I first shut off the main water valve to the house, then start disassembling the plumbing fixtures (mixing valve and shower head, etc.). The door is closed and the fan turned on to keep dust out of the house. I always cut the drywall along the outside edge of the unit with a knife, hammer and chisel to avoid damaging the drywall outside the shower stall. Next, I put on a dust mask and safety glasses, stick a new wood-cutting blade in a reciprocating saw and start cutting from the top, working down. It helps to have someone hold some of the loose pieces, which vibrate as they are cut free from the rest of the unit. Each piece that's carted away makes it easier to attack the remaining section; usually the unit comes out in five or six pieces. The hardest piece to remove surrounds the drain; here, practicing a little patience and cutting smaller pieces help. Once I've cut out around the drain, I reach down and undo the drain assembly with a wrench.

Work from the top down. The first cuts are made in the corners to separate the unit's walls from the tub.

It takes only a few cuts. Once the walls are removed, the tub should come out in pieces that are small enough to cart away without scratching walls and woodwork.

TIP

Avoid floods, shocks and breakage. When cutting, watch out for pipes and wires, and check in neighboring rooms for items like mirrors or vases that might vibrate onto the floor.

Plumbing

Relocating the drain for the new pan.

Once the old tub is removed, the drain typically must be moved from the tub end to the center of the new shower pan. After I open the subfloor, the plumber can reroute the drain and vent to the new position.

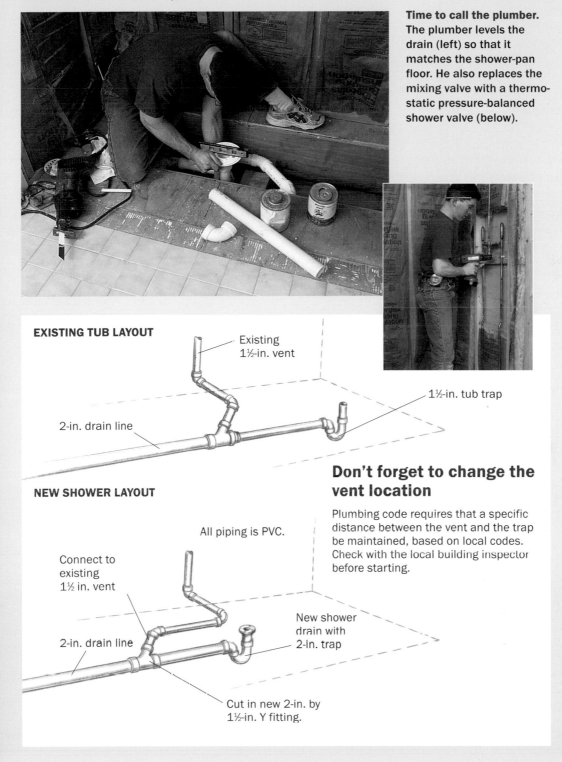

Time to call the plumber. The plumber levels the drain (left) so that it matches the shower-pan floor. He also replaces the mixing valve with a thermostatic pressure-balanced shower valve (below).

EXISTING TUB LAYOUT

Existing 1½-in. vent

1½-in. tub trap

2-in. drain line

NEW SHOWER LAYOUT

All piping is PVC.

Connect to existing 1½ in. vent

2-in. drain line

New shower drain with 2-In. trap

Cut in new 2-in. by 1½-in. Y fitting.

Don't forget to change the vent location

Plumbing code requires that a specific distance between the vent and the trap be maintained, based on local codes. Check with the local building inspector before starting.

Sources

American Standard
800-442-1902
www.americanstandard-us.com
Acrylic/fiberglass shower pans

AquaGlass® Corp.
731-632-2501
www.aquaglass.com

Lasco Bathware
800-94LASCO
www.lascobathware.com

The Noble Co.
800-878-5788
www.noblecompany.com
Chlorinated polyethylene waterproof membrane
Nobleseal® TS

Innovis Corp.
800-382-9653
www.innoviscorp.com
Better Bench™, galvanized-steel seat form

**Laticrete®
International Inc.**
800-243-4788
www.laticrete.com
Thinsets

Bonsal American
800-334-0784
www.bonsal.com
Tile-ready shower pan

Shower Construction

Backer board creates a water-resistant substrate.

Unlike moisture-resistant gypsum-based products, cementitious backer board can't come apart, even if it's soaking wet. Unless the installation is for a commercial steam shower, I don't use a vapor barrier between the framing and the backer board. My experience tells me that any water vapor that does end up in the stud bays won't react with the backer or thinset and will evaporate quickly. Here are a few other tips:

- Use the largest pieces possible. Fewer pieces equals fewer joints, which minimizes any potential for water problems.
- Attach the backer board with 1½-in. galvanized roofing nails or screws, and don't put any fasteners lower than 2 in. above the threshold to avoid leaks.

Securing the backer board. The author likes to nail the substrate every 6 in. to 8 in. (left). All seams are then sealed with fiberglass-mesh tape bedded in thinset and troweled smooth (below).

Shower Pans: Build Your Own or Buy Them Ready Made

I like to build my shower pans with a waterproof membrane and builtup mud floor (see the photo above). I think this type of pan makes the best substrate for a tile floor because it's solid, won't crack, and can conform to fit any space. I usually charge $300 to $400 to build a shower pan, but if you want something faster, you can buy a prefab pan that you still can tile over. Made of waterproof extruded polystyrene and backer board, these pans have floors that slope uniformly to a built-in drain and are relatively easy to install. A 36-in. by 36-in. tile-ready pan by Bonsal American™ (see the top right photo) costs about $400 (see "Sources" on the facing page).

A shower doesn't always have to have a tiled floor and threshold; often, a homeowner just wants a simpler look. Options include prefab shower pans made of fiberglass (see the center right photo) and acrylic (see the bottom right photo) that look fine with most tile jobs. They come in standard sizes that fit many, but not all, installations and are found in most plumbing-

Tile ready: a prefab pan of reinforced backer board.

Fiberglass: inexpensive but the least durable.

Acrylic: a tougher skin than fiberglass.

supply houses and home centers. Expect to pay about $160 for a 32-in. by 32-in. fiberglass pan and about $350 for an acrylic pan of the same size.

The Details: Make a Tile Shower Sparkle

The difference between an average tile job and an outstanding one is often a matter of a few relatively inexpensive details that don't require lots of time but can really personalize the bath area.

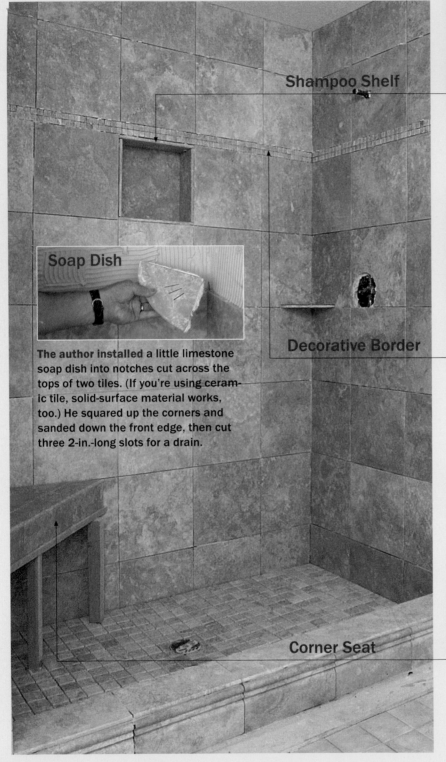

Shampoo Shelf

Soap Dish

The author installed a little limestone soap dish into notches cut across the tops of two tiles. (If you're using ceramic tile, solid-surface material works, too.) He squared up the corners and sanded down the front edge, then cut three 2-in.-long slots for a drain.

Decorative Border

Corner Seat

When laying out the shampoo shelf, first determine where the full tiles will land to keep tile cuts to a minimum. A vacuum helps remove dust as the backer board is cut.

Used for an accent, small mesh-backed tiles are easier to install if they're first mounted on a piece of waterproof membrane with binding-fortified thinset. The membrane also brings the small tiles flush with the big ones.

Available in different sizes (see "Sources"), the galvanized-steel seat form is screwed into the framing behind the backer board at a height of 18 in. from the floor.

Remove the waste, and then reinforce the opening with 2x scrap material secured to the backer board with construction adhesive and galvanized screws.

After coating the recess with thinset, cover the inside with a piece of waterproof membrane, folding and sealing corners as needed. Prefab inserts are also available.

Starting with the bottom piece, line the recess with tile, followed in order by the back, top and sides. All pieces should be back coated with a layer of thinset.

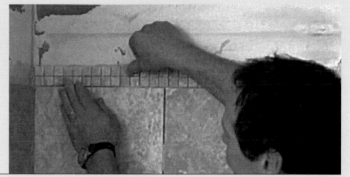

The next day, when the thinset has dried, the assembly is cut into uniform strips two tiles wide and to a length that matches the width of the large tiles.

The strips now can be applied to the backer board with a liberal coating of thinset.

The form then is filled with mud, which creates the substrate for the tile. After the top is leveled off, the mud is left to dry overnight.

After the mud is prepped with successive layers of thinset, waterproof membrane and thinset, tile is laid across the top, then the front. Temporary braces keep the edge tile in place until the thinset bonds.

Tiling a Tub Surround

■ BY MICHAEL BYRNE

Fine tuning. After packing a wall with grout, use a damp sponge to shave high spots and fill voids.

When it comes to low cost and ease of installation, it's hard to beat the fiberglass tub-and-shower unit. It's simply slid into its berth and nailed through the flanges to the framing. When the job is done, everyone gets to bathe and shower in a synthetic shell.

I prefer standard tubs enclosed by tiled walls. Tile is not only peerless in beauty and durability, but it also can be installed with minimal expertise. Whereas tub surrounds once were tiled over skillfully prepared beds of mortar, most tile pros now favor the thin-bed method. It substitutes various prefabricated backer boards for the mortar bed, saving time and trouble without compromising durability. In this chapter I'll explain how to tile a basic tub surround using the thin-bed method. The job shown is a remodel, but the principles apply to new work. To satisfy the design of the room, I did two different edge treatments, one of which mimics the look of a traditional mortar-bed surround.

Framing and Waterproofing

Bathtub bays must be framed plumb, level and square using straight stock. I add extra studs and blocking to support the edges of backer board, plus double studs to support tub enclosures, such as shower doors.

Tub surrounds need a waterproof membrane somewhere between the tile and the framing to prevent moisture infiltration. For this job, I installed economical 15-lb. asphalt felt beneath the backer board.

Before you install felt paper, it's a good idea to mark stud locations with a crayon along the top of the tub so you'll know where to fasten the backer board.

I staple felt to the studs or, if the framing is drywalled, I laminate the felt to the drywall with cold-patch asphalt roofing cement. Adjacent bands of felt are lapped shingle-style to shed water. For insurance, I also seal the joints with asphalt caulk and run a bead of caulk along the top edge of the tub to seal it to the paper.

If I'm working solo, I usually cut the top band of felt paper into two pieces for easier handling. If you do this, lap and seal the vertical joint to keep out water.

Start with a solid frame. Backer board should be affixed to a sturdy and accurately framed wall that includes studs and blocking for the backer-board seams and for the tub enclosure.

Put a membrane under the backer board. The author laps bands of 15-lb. roofing felt, stapled shingle-style to the studs, to keep moisture out of the wall. At vertical seams, he caulks the laps with asphalt to prevent leakage.

Preparing the Backer Board

I've used mesh-reinforced cement board for more than 10 years with excellent results. It has an aggregated portland-cement core with a fiberglass mesh embedded in both sides. Panels range from ¼-in. to ½-in. thick, and they come in various widths and lengths for minimal cutting and easy handling. I sometimes use ¼-in.-thick board over drywall, but I don't use board thinner than ⁷⁄₁₆ in. over bare studs because it's too flimsy.

I cut mesh-reinforced board with a carbide scriber and grind or power sand the edges smooth. I simply mark the cutline, align the straightedge with the mark and score the line with the scriber, making sure I cut through the mesh. Next, the board is flipped over, and the process is repeated. Then I place a straightedge under the full length of the score, grasp the offcut and snap it off. If the offcut is too narrow to snap, I break it off in pieces with tile biters (see "Cutting and Drilling Tiles" on p. 19).

To make small plumbing holes in mesh-reinforced board, I use a carbide-tipped hole saw. For large holes, I'll mark the opening, drill a series of ¼-in. holes around the perimeter, cut through the mesh on both sides, punch through with a hammer and then smooth the edge of the hole with a rasp.

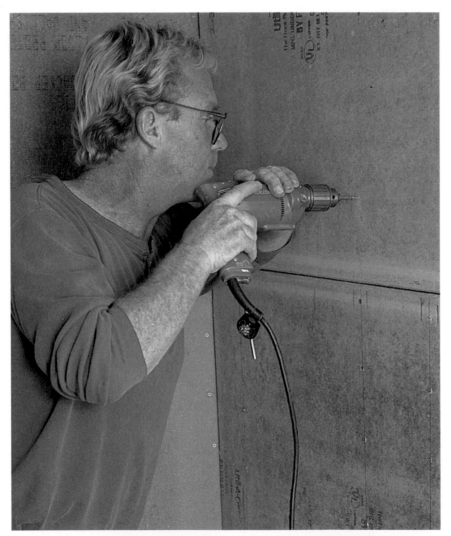

Anchor the backer board. You can use nails to affix backer board to the studs, but the board can be damaged during installation. Corrosion-proof screws are a better choice.

Installing the Backer Board

Backer board can be hung with nails, but I prefer to use screws. They hold better than nails and put less stress on the boards during installation. I avoid regular drywall screws because their heads can snap off and because the screws can rust in a wet tub surround. I used Durock® screws for this job. They come with a corrosion-resistant coating and built-in countersinks that help bury the heads flush with the panel.

I hang backer board on the back wall first, then the side walls, holding the bottom course about ¼ in. off the tub to prevent water from wicking into the board and to allow room for caulk. To speed installation, I start each screw by tapping it with a hammer before I drive it home with a power screwdriver. I space the screws according to the board manufacturer's fastening schedule and provide the recommended expansion gaps around panels.

For a contemporary look, end-wall backer board can be installed flush with adjacent drywall to allow the use of low-profile, surface-bullnose trim tiles (flat tiles with one edge rounded over). But I prefer to install the board so that it stands ½ in. proud, allowing the use of radius-bullnose trim to

Tape the joints. Press self-adhering, fiberglass-mesh tape over the joints, applying three overlapping strips at inside corners.

Fill tape with thinset mortar. Use a trowel to spread thinset mortar over taped joints, forcing the mortar into the fabric of the mesh.

create the classic, curved look usually associated with mortar-bed work. To produce the ½-in. step, you either fur out the backer board or run drywall under it.

Backer board joints get finished with 2-in.- or 4-in.-wide adhesive-backed fiberglass-mesh tape. In corners, I apply three overlapping strips of tape (see the left photo above). Then I trowel the same thinset mortar over the tape that will be used for setting tiles (see the right photo above). I like to finish the joints just before I set the tiles to avoid mixing an extra batch of mortar and to avoid tiling over a thinset ridge that should have been flattened but is now a chunk of stone.

Tile Layout

The ideal layout for tiled tub surrounds produces a symmetrical appearance with minimal cutting. I start by aligning several tiles along a straightedge on the floor with a ⅛-in. spacer in each joint. Although many tiles have integral spacing lugs, they typically

create a grout joint that's only ¹⁄₁₆ in. wide, which I think is weak looking. I like ⅛-in.-wide grout joints because they're stronger and look crisp and clean. Tile spacers—X-shaped pieces of plastic—are available in various widths from any tile store. The number of tiles represents the longest run I'll have to tile—typically the distance from the top of the tub to the ceiling. I stretch a tape from one end of the tiles and record the distance to each joint. Correlating these numbers with actual wall dimensions allows me to plan my cuts before tiling.

Back walls usually look best with identical vertical rows of cut tiles at each end. I mark the vertical centerline of the wall, plumb a level to it and scribe a pencil line on the backer board from tub to ceiling. When laying the tile, I'll work out from the centerline in both directions. End walls need one vertical line to mark the outboard edge of the field tiles. On this job, the plumbing wall would require one vertical row of cut tiles, which could be placed in the front or in the rear. Because the opposite wall would

Measure the tiles. To plan tile cuts, space a row of tiles along a straightedge, measure the distance from the end of the row to each joint and correlate the measurements with actual wall dimensions.

have full tiles all the way across, I chose to put full tiles in the back to match and to cut trim tiles at the front.

Instead of drawing horizontal layout lines on the wall, I level a straightedge above the rim of the tub with shims (unless the tub is level enough to work off of, which is rare). I tile from the straightedge to the ceiling, remove the straightedge and then fill in the bottom courses. Horizontal rows of cut tiles can be placed against the tub, the ceiling or both, depending on personal preference (I put them against the ceiling on this job). They also can take the form of a decorative band somewhere in between.

Mixing and Spreading Mortar

Tiles can be bedded in mastic, but you'll get better results using thinset mortar. It's a mortar-based adhesive that's mixed with water, epoxy resin or a liquid latex or acrylic additive that increases bond strength, compressive strength and flexibility. I use thinset mortar mixed with 4237 liquid latex mortar additive (both made by Laticrete International Inc.). If you're worried about fussing with too many ingredients, use a powdered thinset that includes a dry polymer additive and is mixed with water. Regardless of the mortar you use, don't mix it without donning a dust mask, safety glasses and rubber gloves. For best results,

Wrong trowel. Determine the right trowel-notch size by spreading mortar on a small patch of wall. Then, comb the mortar with the trowel and firmly press the tile into the mortar. Pull the tile away and assess the coverage. There shouldn't be any bare spots. This test was done with a ¼-in. by ¼-in. trowel.

Right trowel. Minimal squeeze-out and complete coverage on the back of this tile denote a properly sized and notched trowel for applying mortar. If mortar had oozed from the edges of this test tile, the author would have switched to smaller notches. This test was done with a ¼-in. by ⅜-in. trowel.

the temperature at the job site should be between 65°F and 75°F.

Although professional installers use power mixers, the strongest mortars are mixed by hand. Hand mixing doesn't infuse air into the mortar as some power mixers do. I begin by pouring all of the liquid and

about 75 percent of the recommended amount of thinset powder into a clean bucket. Using a margin trowel, I mix until most of the lumps are gone. Then, I add half of the remaining powder, mix, add the other half and mix again. You have to let the material slake (rest) for 5 minutes to 10 minutes, then mix the batch once more until it's lump-free and ready to apply. The batch now should be plastic but not runny. I'm careful not to expose the mortar to direct sunlight (which can cook it) or to excessive air-conditioning (which can dry it out). At this point, the mortar should be wet enough to adhere to any surface instantly but not slip easily off the trowel.

Before applying mortar to the backer board, I wipe the board with a damp sponge to remove dust. I apply mortar with a standard notched trowel using the smooth edge to spread the mortar on the substrate and the notched edges to comb the mortar into uniform ridges. The notch size depends on the size of the tile, the condition of the substrate and the type of adhesive you are using. The general recommendation is to use a notch two-thirds the depth of the tile. The best way to select the proper trowel, however, is to test it with the first tile you set.

Setting Field Tiles

Bathtubs that are used constantly should be tiled with vitreous tiles, which are virtually waterproof. This tub is a backup, so I used standard 4¼-in. wall tiles having a soft, thin glaze and a porous, chalky bisque (the clay beneath the surface). They are less expensive than vitreous tiles, and they are easier to cut.

I tile the back wall one quadrant at a time, followed by the bottom half and top half of each end wall. Beginning at the back wall, I shim a straightedge to provide a level work surface above the tub. Then, I trowel mortar over an entire section above it (see the left photo on p. 18). I apply the mortar

Spreading mortar. Use the straight edge of the notched trowel to spread thinset mortar. Use the notched edge to comb uniform ridges.

Setting the tiles. With the bottom of the tile resting on spacer blocks, the author tilts each tile onto the mortar and then presses it home.

in a thick, relatively uniform layer, and I press hard to key it into the pores of the backer board. That done, I comb the mortar with the notched trowel, maintaining constant contact with the board and keeping the angle of the trowel consistent to produce ridges that are uniform.

I set the first row of tiles along the straightedge. I position the bottom edge of each tile first, then tilt it forward into the mortar (a process I call "hinging"). Then I slip a spacer between each tile, adjusting the spacing of the tiles as needed. On subsequent courses, I hinge the tiles off the spacers (see the photo above right). I lay all full tiles in a section first, then fill in any cut tiles. If the mortar skins over before a section is finished, you should recomb it. If you break the initial set by moving a tile, scrape the mortar off the tile and the substrate and apply fresh mortar. I keep a wet sponge handy for wiping goo off the surface of tiles before it hardens.

After I've tiled all the sections on a wall and all the adhesive has set up, I remove the straightedge and install the bottom courses of tile, taping them temporarily to the tiles above to prevent sagging. Because I apply

mortar carefully, I don't have to seat the tiles with the traditional beating block (a padded block of wood or plywood that's laid over tiles and rapped with a rubber mallet). Instead, I use one to coax tiles gently into a smooth plane.

To enliven this surround, I installed a liner at about eye level. A liner is a decorative horizontal stripe of tile, usually less than 1 in. wide, that's used to interrupt a field of tiles. Stock liners are available in unlimited sizes and colors, but I cut my own out of matching or slightly contrasting field and trim tiles. In some cases, liners can eliminate the need to install horizontal rows of cut tiles against the ceiling or tub.

Setting Trim Tiles

Surface-bullnose trim tiles are cut and installed just as field tiles, then temporarily taped to neighboring tiles to prevent sagging (see the left photo on the facing page). To install radius-bullnose trim tiles, I apply a skin coat of thinset mortar to the backer board and to the flat part of the tile backs. Then, I butter the curves on the tile backs with the same grout I use for tile joints

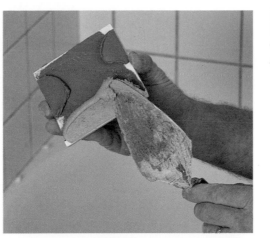

Butter the backs. For radius-bullnose trim, spread mortar on the flat part of the tile and grout on the curved part.

Prevent sagging trim. Keep the trim tiles from drooping as they set up by taping them temporarily to the field tiles. These are surface-bullnose tiles, which are used to end a row of tile when the backer board and the adjacent wall are in the same plane.

Look for squeeze-out. Press radius-bullnose tiles firmly enough so that grout oozes out. Remove the excess before it hardens.

(see the top right photo above). A small amount of grout should squeeze out the ends of each tile as I push it home (see the bottom right photo above). I lay the whole row, then nudge it into alignment with a straightedge, gently tapping the tiles flat with the trowel handle and applying tape to prevent sagging. When the grout begins to solidify, I pare the edge square to the drywall with the margin trowel.

Cutting and Drilling Tiles

The snap cutter, which you can rent from many tile stores and tool-rental shops, is the tool to use for cutting tiles down to ½ in. wide. I mark cutlines on the tiles with a fine-point, felt-tip pen, then score and break the tiles with the cutter. I then ease the resulting sharp edges with a tile-rubbing stone.

Biters are used primarily for trimming tiles to fit around plumbing (see the top photo on p. 20). They have a curved cutting edge on one side and a straight one on the other that bites into the glazed side of the tile. To make holes in the middle of tiles, I use a carbide-tipped hole saw.

For removing less than ½ in. from tiles, you have to score the tiles with the snap cutter, then nibble to the line with a pair of biters, working in from the corners of the tiles to prevent breakage. And, again, you would smooth the raw edges with a rubbing stone. To make a tile less than ½ in. wide requires a wet saw.

Grouting

Tile spacers come in various thicknesses, and some are thin enough that you can grout right over them. I prefer the thicker spacers, and I pull them out (using a dental pick) after the thinset cures. Once I've removed

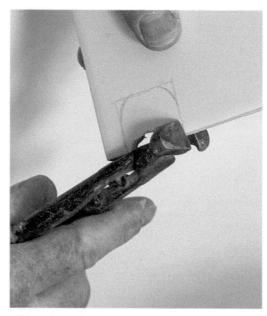

Nibble the notches. Use a biter to notch tiles around plumbing, working in from the corners of the notch to prevent unwanted breakage.

all the tile spacers and globs of thinset mortar from the joints, I'm ready to grout. I check the thinset container to see if there's a waiting period. If so, I wait, or the thinset mortar might stain the grout.

I use a powdered polymer-modified grout called Polyblend® from Custom Building Products, which is mixed with water. It comes in 47 colors, and the company sells caulks to match.

Only the rubber face of a grout trowel can pack joints full without scratching tiles (see the bottom photo at left). I start with the back wall and use the trowel to spread grout over a small section. I tilt the trowel to a 40-degree angle or less and work the grout into the joints (see the photo below). I attack joints from three directions, with each pass cramming more grout into the joint until it's completely filled. Once all the joints in a section are filled, I hold the trowel at a right angle to the surface and rake it diagonally along the tiles to scrape off excess grout (see the top left photo on the facing page). I grout the entire wall this way, packing everything except for the expansion joint above the tub and gaps around plumbing fixtures. Because grout will stiffen in the bucket, it should be stirred occasionally.

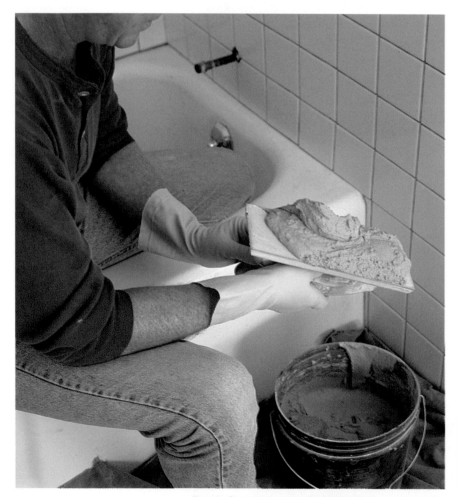

Ready for grout. Load freshly mixed grout onto the rubber face of a grout trowel.

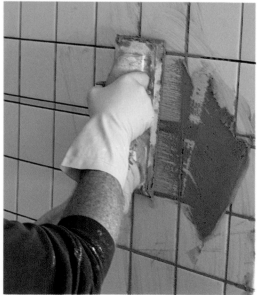

Pack the grout. Hold the trowel at a slight angle and spread grout over a small section. Work grout into the joints until they are full.

Next, I thoroughly wring out a wet, rounded sponge and gently wipe the freshly packed wall in a circular motion to shave off high spots. I avoid feathering the grout over the edges of the tiles. Then, I complete the wet cleaning by making 3-ft.-long parallel swipes with the damp sponge, using a clean face for each swipe (see the bottom photo). At this point, I rinse the sponge after every two swipes.

Remove the excess. Hold the trowel nearly perpendicular to the wall and scrape off the excess grout with the edge of the trowel.

Wet cleanup. Complete wet cleaning by making parallel strokes with a damp sponge, using a clean side of the sponge per wipe.

Dry cleanup. About 15 minutes after sponging, wipe off grout haze with a dry cloth, leaving the surround ready for sealing and caulking.

About 15 minutes later, grout haze should be visible on the surface of the tile. I remove it by rubbing the tiles with a soft cloth or cheesecloth. If that doesn't work, I'll try a damp sponge or white Scotch-Brite® pad. At this stage, with the grout set up, I use a utility knife to remove the grout from the corner joint and from the ¼-in. joint I left between the tile and the tub. These expansion joints need to be filled with sealant.

After all grouting and cleaning is completed, I let the job rest while the grout cures and dries (usually about 72 hours). Then, I return to seal the grout and the raw edges of the tile with an impregnator. I use 511 Impregnator® made by the Miracle Sealants & Abrasives Company®. You have to allow the impregnator to dry before you caulk the expansion joints around the tub. I use a sealant that can be color matched to the tile, the grout or the plumbing fixture. It is available either sanded or unsanded (Pro-Line Class A Sealant from Color Caulk Inc.).

Michael Byrne is the author of Setting Tile, *published by The Taunton Press, Inc.*

Sources

U.S. Gypsum
125 S. Franklin St.
Chicago, IL 60606
800-874-4968
www.usg.com
Durock screws

Laticrete International Inc.
1 Laticrete Park N
Bethany, CT 06524
800-243-4788
www.laticrete.com

Custom Building Products
6511 Salt Lake Ave.
Bell, CA 90201
323-582-0846
www.cbp.com
Polyblend

Miracle Sealants Co.
12318 Lower Azusa Rd.
Arcadia, CA 91006
800-350-1901
www.miracle-sealants.com
511 Impregnator

Roanoke Companies Group.
1105 S. Frontenac St.
Aurora, IL 60504
800-552-6225
www.colorcaulk.com
ProLine Class A Sealant

Tiling a Shower with Marble

■ BY TOM MEEHAN

A showy shower out of stone. Before installation, marble tiles are arranged so that the veins and colorations all work together. The tiles are put on as flat as possible and tight to one another to give the impression of a solid slab of marble.

<B>ack a few hundred million years or so, Earth was working overtime. Incredible forces and pressures within the planet moved continents and created mountains. Limestone, formed from the skeletons and shells of countless sea creatures, underwent an intense and miraculous transformation during this period. The result of this metamorphosis is marble, which has become a prized building material.

While marble was being formed, various minerals and contaminants were introduced, producing the veins and rich colors that make each batch of marble unique. However, all of these wonderful colors make installing marble an interesting challenge. In 25 years as a tile installer, I have learned the importance of opening every box of marble and shuffling the tiles to get the veins and colors to work together before a project begins. My goal is to blend the tiles in such a way that the finished shower wall resembles a solid slab of marble.

The project in this article is a 7-ft. by 3½-ft. shower stall with a built-in seat and a shampoo shelf. The shower-door enclosure runs the full 7 ft. along the front of the shower bay with 1-ft. returns on both ends (see the photo on the facing page). This arrangement shows off the entire expanse of marble. For this particular shower, my clients chose green marble, which needs special treatment because of its chemical makeup. Green-marble tile reacts negatively to water-based or acrylic thinset cement, causing the tile to warp and break down. I avoid these problems by sealing the back of each tile with epoxy before it is installed, which I will describe in detail later on.

Backer Board Must be Kept off the Floor

Marble tiles for any shower should be mounted on cement backer board. For this project I used Durock (see "Sources" on p. 29), which consists of a thin layer of cement sandwiched between two layers of fiberglass mesh.

Even though backer board is not supposed to deteriorate or fall apart, it is a porous material and must be kept off the bottom of the shower floor to prevent moisture from wicking up the wall (see the photo above). If the backer board gets wet, it can stain the marble tile from behind. I usually keep it around 1½ in. from the floor. I also keep the nails in my backer board above the top of the shower pan or at least 5 in. from the floor to prevent the shower pan from leaking. Installing the backer board too low and nailing through the shower pan are probably the two most frequent causes of failure with a marble-tile installation in a shower.

Cutting and installing the backer board is a lot like hanging drywall, except that all of my straight cuts are done with a special backer board knife with a carbide blade. These knives are available for under $10 at your local tile store or at any lumberyard that sells cement backer board. I treat backer board the same as a piece of drywall, making three or four long strikes along a straightedge and then bending the sheet back and slicing the mesh on the back with a utility knife. For cutting right angles or corners, I use my grinder with a 4-in. diamond blade. Grinder cutting creates a lot of dust, so I wear a respirator and try to cut outside whenever possible.

Keeping the backer board off the floor will save headaches later. A 2x4 block is used as a spacer to hold the backer board off the shower floor. If installed too low, backer board can soak up moisture that will stain the marble from behind.

A hammer works like a hole saw. The quickest, easiest way to make a hole in backer board is to pulverize the unwanted cement by tapping it with a hammer. A utility knife can be used to cut the mesh away from both sides of the board.

Small holes in backer board can be drilled with a carbide-tipped hole saw. But large holes for the mixing valve and pipes are made a little differently (see the photo above). First I map out where I want the board removed. Then I tap at the board with a hammer until the area inside my lines has been reduced to cement dust with just the mesh on both sides holding it in place. At this point, I cut away the mesh with a utility knife and remove the pulverized cement.

Before installing the board, I check the studs with a straightedge to make sure they are all in the same plane. If need be, I build out any studs that are out of line to keep the backer board as flat as possible. The backer board gets nailed to the wall every 8 in. with 1½-in. galvanized ring-shank nails. I also put in a few galvanized screws along the seams for extra reinforcement. With the board nailed in place, I finish the seams with mesh tape and thinset mortar to seal the joints and prevent future cracking and settling.

Green Marble Needs to Be Sealed with Epoxy before Installation

Most marble can be put directly on the wall with regular thinset mortar, but as I mentioned before, green marble is apt to warp and break down. Adhesive manufacturers recommend that green marble be set directly on the wall with epoxy mortar, but this procedure requires large quantities of epoxy, which is very expensive. A different solution that I've used successfully is sealing the backs of the green-marble tiles with epoxy and installing them with less expensive thinset mixed with the proper additive (see the photo on the facing page).

Epoxy seals the backs of the green-marble tiles. Green marble reacts badly to water-based adhesives, so the backs of the tiles are sealed with nonporous epoxy. A trowel spreads the thick and gooey epoxy.

I use an epoxy product made by Laticrete International Inc. (see "Sources"). The three-part mixture comes conveniently in a can with a pair of disposable gloves and a white scrub pad for warm-water cleanup. Working with epoxy is something akin to working with saltwater taffy—sticky, messy and tedious. So I make an extra effort to keep this part of the operation as neat and orderly as possible. Using a flat trowel, I skim-coat the back of each tile with a thin layer of epoxy. Then I stand the tiles upright and on edge to dry, just barely touching each other.

After giving the epoxy 24 hours to dry, I scrape all of the tiles' edges with a sharp utility knife to remove any excess. Cleaning the edges will ensure that the tiles will fit together tightly when they are installed.

Once the backs of the marble tiles have been coated with epoxy, the proper thinset must be used to bond the tiles to the walls and floor. Plain thinset or thinset with a basic acrylic additive is fine for regular marble and might seem to work initially for the epoxy-coated tiles as well. But the longevity of a bond between regular thinset and epoxy is questionable. The thinset must be mixed with an additive specifically designed for bonding to a resilient surface such as vinyl or linoleum flooring. This mixture will also bond to the nonporous epoxy coating on the marble. MAPEI® and Laticrete both make good products for this application (see "Sources").

A Ledger Board Starts the Tiles Out Level

The two main objectives when installing marble tile are keeping the joints between tiles tight and making the walls a continuous, flat, even plane.

I took great pains ahead of time to build this shower stall in even 12-in. increments. This careful planning kept my cut tiles close to full size. I laid out the shower with full-width tile for the top course against the ceiling and cut tile on the bottom course along the floor. Rather than begin my tile installation with the cut course, however, I opted to start with the first course of full-width tiles. To keep this starter course perfectly level, I tacked a ledger board on the wall along the bottom edge of the course of tile (see the photo on p. 26). This ledger board also provided some support for the heavy marble tiles while the adhesive was curing.

I began by spreading my thinset mixture on the walls with a ⅜-in. notched trowel, covering enough of the wall for two courses. Then I buttered the back of each tile before it went on the wall. With this amount of thinset, I can push a tile in or build it out as needed to keep the wall perfectly flat. Two tools that come in handy for this process are a rubber mallet and a large suction cup with a release switch, available at tile stores, glass shops or marble-supply stores. I use the mallet to tap tiles in and to keep them tight to one another, and the suction cup lets me pull a tile out and reset it if it's in too far.

A ledger board keeps the starter course level. A length of 1× is leveled and tacked to the wall to provide support and alignment for the starting course of tile.

Keep in mind that, unlike ceramic tile, marble has a square outside edge that becomes visible with the slightest bit of unevenness in the installation. After setting the first three courses on the back wall, I moved to the side walls to give the thinset a chance to set a little before adding the weight of the additional courses.

Simple Cuts and a Complementary Color Create a Decorative Border

To minimize the cold, formal look a large marble shower stall can sometimes have, my client decided to add a decorative band just above the fifth course of tile (see the photo on p. 22). To create this border, I used my wet saw to cut a bunch of the sealed green

Thinner tiles are used to build out the decorative band. Full-size tiles are cut into smaller squares, then cut in half again. A complementary color was chosen for the diamond. Instead of giving these smaller tiles a thick bed of mortar, thin and unglazed tiles were used to shim them out to the plane of the rest of the wall.

tiles and several beige marble tiles into 4-in. squares. Then I cut each of the 4-in. green tiles in half diagonally and created a two-tone diamond band that runs around the perimeter of the shower. At the corners of the shower stall, I used half of a beige diamond going in both directions to give the appearance of a folded tile.

Building these small tiles out to the same plane as the rest of the wall can present a problem. I had used a fairly thick layer of adhesive to keep the 12-in. by 12-in. tiles flat. This method can get pretty sloppy and difficult when building out small tiles. So I used some leftover unglazed mosaic tiles as shims to bring the decorative pieces out flush with the field tiles (see the photo above). The thinset adhesive had no problem adhering to mosaic tile because both sides of the tile were unglazed.

Bullnosing the Tiles Can Be Done with a Saw and a Grinder

I bullnosed, or rounded the edges of, all of the tiles for the outside corners of the shower stall to soften the edge. I own a water-fed router, but it was in the repair shop when I was working on this project. Because the router is both wet and loud, I try to use it only if I have a lot of bullnosing to do. Instead of the router, I used another method that's a bit slower and requires a little more patience. But I find it gives the same great results.

First I run a tile through my tile saw, holding it at a 45-degree angle, removing only about ⅛ in. from the edge of the tile. After making this cut on several tiles, I set up five or six in a row on the edge of a table or bench. I use a grinder or spin sander with 80-grit paper to round off the two edges of the chamfer and create the bullnose on all five tiles at once. Then I polish the rounded edge with sanding disks, working progressively up to 600 grit.

Diamond pads soaked in water can also be used to create the bullnose after chamfering. These pads make less dust and work better on marble than regular sanding disks. Diamond pads come as a six-part, color-keyed, graduated-grit system that can be purchased from most marble-supply houses. When I've worked through the finest grit, I rub a little marble polish on the bullnose as a final step.

Tiling is tough on tools. A framing square is used to check the alignment of the floor tiles and to keep them running straight. But it's hard to do without plunking the tool down in fresh adhesive, which isn't great for the square.

Smaller Tiles Conform to the Slope of the Shower Floor

It's possible but not practical to use 12-in. tile on the shower floor. So again I cut full-size tiles into 4-in. squares. Using smaller tiles not only makes it easier to match the gradual pitch of the shower pan, but it also increases the number of grout joints for better traction on the slippery marble surface.

I spread my thinset on the floor with a ¼-in. notched trowel for the smaller floor tiles. Because of the slope of the shower floor and the ample size of the grout joints, I didn't need to butter the backs of the tiles with thinset. To add a little character to the floor, I used triangular tiles around the perimeter, which put the field tile on the diagonal. Because the shower floor was so large, I checked my rows of tile often with a framing square and a straightedge to keep everything straight and even (see the photo above).

A Corner Seat and Shampoo Shelf Are Built into the Shower Walls

When I was installing the backer board for the shower seat, I extended it 1½ in. higher than the top of the framing, which was covered with the waterproof membrane. Instead of putting backer board on top of the seat, I filled the extra 1½ in. with a bed of cement so that there would be no nails directly under the horizontal surface of the seat (see the photo on the facing page). This technique is a great way to avoid both staining and leaks down the road.

I also gave the cement a good ¼-in. pitch away from the walls so that water would run off the seat easily. Instead of tiles, I used a marble slab that I got from a marble supplier for the top of the seat. The solid piece of marble not only looks better than a course of tiles but also provides seamless waterproofing for one of the most vulnerable areas of the shower stall. The top of the shower threshold received a similar treatment.

The marble for the seat goes on top of cement. The backer board around the shower seat was left 1½ in. high, and then the resulting cavity was filled with cement, making the seat top virtually waterproof. A marble slab was used for the seat to eliminate grout joints.

I laid out the built-in shampoo shelf after I installed the first three courses of tile so that the shelf would land directly above a full-tile course. I cut the opening for the shelf in the backer board with my grinder. The shelf cavity was framed with lengths of 2x4s that I stuck in with dabs of mastic. The mastic held the framing in place until I could screw through the board to attach the framing permanently. As I did with the seat, I pitched the shelf to shed water, but not enough to let the shampoo bottles slide out.

Clean Marble with a pH-Neutral Solution

After the marble was installed, I grouted the whole shower with a forest green grout. It's a good idea to test the grout on a tile scrap to make sure that it won't stain the marble. I mixed my grout the way I usually do, using plain water, and I spread the grout with a float and a stiff, damp sponge. Even though the wall tiles are a tight fit, I go over them to fill any hairline gaps that might be left. The grout joints between the marble floor tiles are filled the same as for ceramic tile.

I give grout a couple of days to cure before I clean the tile. Marble is sensitive to acid, so it must be cleaned with a pH-neutral cleaning solution. There are several marble cleaners on the market, and they're available

at most tile stores. Avoid acidic cleaners such as vinegar, which can etch the surface of the tile and strip it of its finish. I give the marble a final rinse with clean water even after using a cleaner made for marble.

Most marble in a heavily used shower will require maintenance. Lighter marble is particularly vulnerable to staining, but all marble needs to be kept properly sealed. Two weeks after the installation, I seal the marble with an impregnator/sealer called Stand Off® Limestone & Marble Protector made by ProSoCo (see "Sources"). This product seals the microscopic pores of the stone. It doesn't change the appearance of the marble, but it helps repel water and prevent deep staining.

I always test the sealer on a scrap of whatever marble I've used in a project. It's best to leave it overnight to make sure there are no adverse chemical reactions on the surface of the marble.

Finally, I go over the shower walls with marble polish, which offers additional protection from soap and shampoo and gives the marble a nice, even finish.

Tom Meehan is a second-generation tile installer, owner of Cape Cod Tileworks in Harwich, Massachusetts, and co-author of Build Like a Pro® Working With Tile *(The Taunton Press, Inc., 2005).*

Sources

Laticrete International Inc.
1 Laticrete Park N
Bethany, CT 06524
800-243-4788

MAPEI Inc.
1350 Lively Blvd.
Elk Grove Village, IL. 60007
South River, NJ 08882
800-426-2734
www.mapei.com/mapeiamericas

ProSoCo
3741 Greenway Circle
Lawrence, KS 66046
800-255-4255
www.prosoco.com
Stand Off

United States Gypsum Co.
125 S. Franklin St.
Chicago, IL 60606
800-874-4968
Durock

Tiling a Bathroom Floor

■ BY DENNIS HOURANY

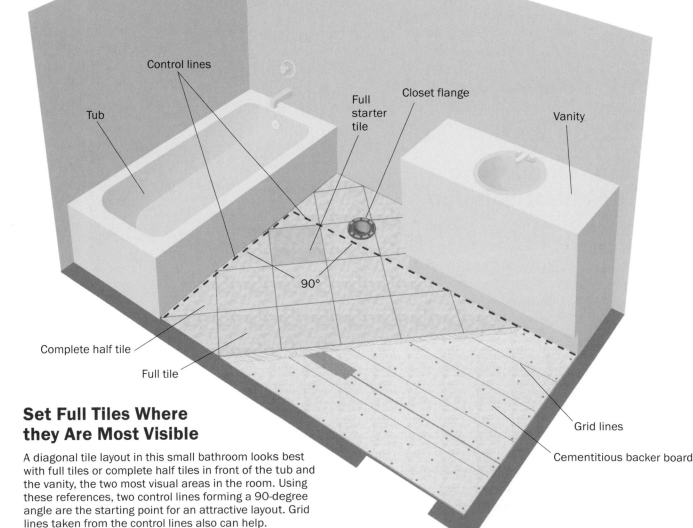

Control lines

Tub

Full starter tile

Closet flange

Vanity

90°

Complete half tile

Full tile

Grid lines

Cementitious backer board

Set Full Tiles Where they Are Most Visible

A diagonal tile layout in this small bathroom looks best with full tiles or complete half tiles in front of the tub and the vanity, the two most visual areas in the room. Using these references, two control lines forming a 90-degree angle are the starting point for an attractive layout. Grid lines taken from the control lines also can help.

If anything can beat ceramic tile for a bathroom floor, I'd like to know what it is. Durable and nearly impervious to water damage, tile also is adaptable to just about any architectural style. The ceramic-tile industry now offers an incredible variety of tile as well as reliable materials for setting it. If tile is more expensive than some other floor coverings, keep in mind that it can last as long as the house with little upkeep.

True enough, but a tile floor can be a nightmare if it is not laid out and installed carefully on a well-prepared subfloor. One of the key early considerations is the substrate on which the tile will be installed. Floating a mortar bed at least 1¼ in. thick used to be the only choice, but now there's a better option: quick-to-install cementitious backer board.

As for the tile itself, durability and smoothness are of major concern. Most tile manufacturers rate their tiles for durability by classifying them as residential, commercial, light industrial or industrial. For a bathroom at home, the residential grade is just fine. Smoothness is rated on a numerical scale measuring the coefficient of friction, or COF. Even though the roughness scale goes all the way to 9, I've found that a rating of 0.6 provides good slip resistance. Just keep in mind, though, that the COF goes down when the tile is wet. If you don't find the COF specified on the tile box, you can call the manufacturer for the information.

Make Sure the Subfloor Is Flat

Setting tile on an inadequate subfloor is begging for trouble. The subfloor should meet deflection criteria set by the Tile Council of America (see "Sources" on p. 39)—in other

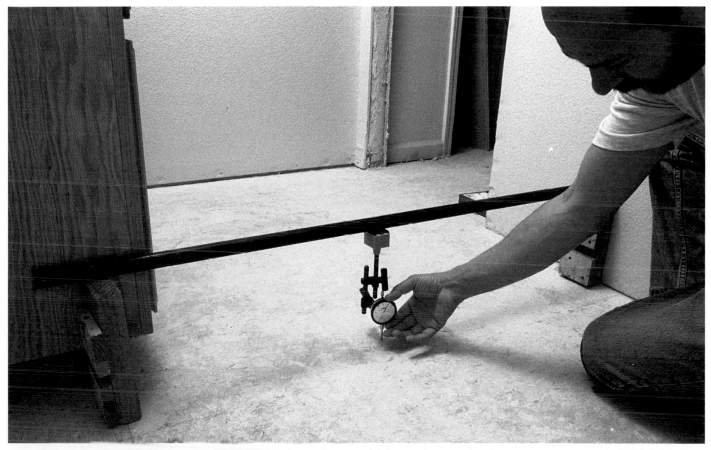

Is the floor stiff enough? A dial indicator attached to a length of iron pipe is one way to check whether there is too much deflection in the subfloor. A bouncy subfloor will result in cracked tile or grout.

words, it can't have too much bounce. If it does, chances are good that the tile will lose its bond with the backer board or that the grout joints between the tiles will crack at the very least. The Tile Council allows a maximum deflection of $\frac{1}{360}$ of the span, or the span in inches divided by 360. For example, if you have a span of 48 in., the most sag the subfloor can show under a load is 0.13 in., or roughly $\frac{1}{8}$ in. Although the Tile Council calls for a minimum $\frac{5}{8}$-in. exterior-grade plywood subfloor, houses where I've set tile often have subfloors of $\frac{5}{8}$-in. oriented strand board, and I haven't had any problems. Minimum joist spacing is 16 in. on center (o.c.)

I can sense whether there's too much bounce simply by walking around on a floor. That's after setting hundreds of tile floors. When I started, though, I measured the deflection with a length of iron pipe and a dial indicator just to make sure (see the photo on p. 31). If there's too much deflection, don't go any further without fixing the problem.

The subfloor also must be flat. Here, the maximum amount of leeway is $\frac{1}{8}$ in. in 10 ft. That means if you were to lay a straightedge on the subfloor, you should not be able to see a hump or a dip that exceeds $\frac{1}{8}$ in. A wavy floor can be corrected. One way is to use a leveling compound over the wood subfloor before the backer board is installed. You can also put the backer board down first and then use a leveling compound that bonds to it.

In either case, the application is the same. Using a straightedge, pull some leveling compound across the low spots to fill them in. You may need to use more than one application. Leveling compounds are typically available from tile suppliers.

When Installing Backer Board, Don't Forget to Leave an Expansion Gap

Cementitious backer board is made by several manufacturers and is readily available. I use $\frac{1}{4}$-in. HardiBacker® (see "Sources"). Sheets come in several sizes. I like this product a lot more than the backer board with fiberglass mesh on each side. HardiBacker cuts cleanly and easily (see the photo below), and it's simple to fasten to the subfloor. The $\frac{1}{4}$-in. thickness makes it easy to keep the tile at the right height, without framing a recess into the floor or having an awkward lip

The author uses HardiBacker, a ¼-in. cementitious backer board, as a tile substrate. Scored on one side with a carbide tool, the board will snap cleanly with no back cut.

Glue for the backer board. The author uses a type I mastic to bond the backer board to the oriented-strand-board sub-floor. An acrylic-modified thin-set mortar also could be used.

Nail it down. Galvanized roofing nails 1¼ in. long should be driven 6 in. o.c. to install the backer board. Set the nail heads flush with the surface.

where the tile meets another floor surface. However, if you need to raise the level of the floor to meet an adjoining surface, you could use ½-in. cement board.

I cut and lay out the entire floor's backer board before nailing any down. When it's laid out, joints should be staggered and edges should overlap subfloor joints. It is imperative that you leave a ⅛-in. expansion gap between sheets and a ¼-in. gap at perimeter walls or other restraining surfaces, such as cabinets.

Most manufacturers require that the backer board be bonded to the subfloor with an adhesive, and I use type I mastic. You can use thinset adhesive, but the mastic works just as well in this application, and it's faster and easier to apply (check with the backer board manufacturer before deciding what to use). Whatever the adhesive, put it down evenly with the notched trowel recommended by the manufacturer, and don't

Cut crucial tile while the floor is dry. Before applying thinset to the backer board, the author lays out the floor and cuts tiles to go around obstructions, such as this closet flange.

A wet saw works best. A tile saw is the most versatile tool for cutting tile. Curved cuts start with a series of straight cuts to the layout line.

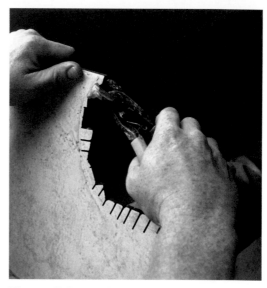

Nippers finish the job. After the author makes a rough curved cut with a wet saw, he removes the waste with tile nippers.

apply any more adhesive than can be covered with backer board before it skins over (see the top photo on p. 33).

I also use 1¼-in. galvanized roofing nails driven into the backer board every 6 in. (see the bottom photo on p. 33). Nail heads should be flush with the backer board, and if the floor is anything but tiny, you'll find a pneumatic nailer is a big help. I don't use screws because HardiBacker does not require them and they're much slower to install.

Set Control Lines for Laying the Tile, and Cut the Odd Ducks

When beginning a layout, I start by checking that walls are square and parallel. If you find things are seriously out of whack and will cause many small tiles or unsightly cuts, you may consider installing the tile on a

diagonal. That's what I did here, although the reason was to add a little interest to the floor, not because the room was out of square. Diagonal layouts also have the effect of making a narrow room appear wider.

Most every room has obvious focal points where full tiles should go. I establish two control lines, 90 degrees to each other, and orient them so that they correspond with the room's focal points. For example, in the small bathroom I'm tiling here, the two critical points are in front of the vanity and in front of the bathtub; I plan on using full tiles (or complete half tiles) in these areas (see the drawing on p. 30). The cut tiles will go where they are less obvious. In general, I try to avoid cutting tiles to less than half their original size—they just look unsightly.

After you've determined the basic layout and the control lines, you can snap grid lines that will guide you as you set the tile. Plastic spacers will keep your grout lines a consistent width. But don't count on them entirely to keep the layout straight because tiles vary somewhat in size. Follow the layout lines, no matter what, for straight grout lines.

I think it's a good idea to cut some tile in advance while the floor is still free of adhesive. I don't cut all of them, just those around the closet flange or other oddly shaped spaces (see the left photo on the facing page). Once you get to a point where full field tiles (or cut tiles of a uniform size) will be used, cutting and fitting them in advance isn't necessary.

To cut tile, I use a tile saw and a pair of nippers (see the right photos on the facing page). You could use a tile board, which works by scoring and snapping tile much as you would cut a piece of glass (these tools also are called snap cutters). One disadvantage of a tile board, though, is that it can't cut L and U shapes. You can use a grinder with a diamond blade or a jigsaw with a Carborundum™ blade to cut tile. However, it's more difficult, and the cuts are not as clean.

You can't go any further without mixing up a batch of thinset mortar, which is used to bridge the seams in the backer board and to glue down the tile. I use acrylic-modified thinset no matter what the substrate. It provides a better bond, offers more flexibility and stays usable in the bucket longer than others. Some kinds of tile require different thinset additives, so be sure to consult with your supplier to make sure that you have the right kind.

Preparing Thinset Requires Precision

When mixing thinset, follow the directions on the bag to the letter. One requirement is that the mixture slake, or rest, in the bucket for 15 minutes after the initial mix. Then mix it again before use. Occasional stirring may help keep the thinset workable, but don't add any more acrylic admix or water much after the second mixing. I use a ½-in. drill to turn a mixing paddle between 300 rpm and 400 rpm (see the photo below).

Taping the joints between pieces of backer board helps prevent cracks later. I use 2-in.-wide fiberglass mesh, bedding it in a layer of thinset (see the top left photo on p. 36). Make sure that the seams between sheets are completely filled. After you apply the first layer of adhesive and tape, you'll need to put down another layer of thinset over the tape with the flat side of a margin trowel, holding it at a 45-degree angle and pressing the tape firmly into the thinset. If you tile the floor in the same day, you can tape as you go so that you won't walk or kneel in wet adhesive. But if you wait overnight, make sure not to leave any lumps of thinset at the seams.

Stir the thinset with a slow-speed paddle. A mixing paddle turning between 300 rpm and 400 rpm does a good job of stirring up a batch of thinset. It needs to be allowed to slake, or rest, for 15 minutes before it can be used to lay tile.

Tape seams now to avoid cracks later. Fiberglass-mesh tape bedded in a thin layer of thinset spans the gap between adjoining sheets of backer board. Skipping the tape can cause cracks to develop later.

Bed the tile in thinset mortar. When you're setting tile, plastic spacers will keep grout joints uniform in width, but following control lines is a better guarantee that grout lines will be straight.

Apply an even layer of thinset. The author uses a notched trowel to spread acrylic-modified thinset for the tile, taking care not to obscure layout lines.

Check the thinset. After setting a few tiles, lift one up to make sure they have enough thinset. Large tiles such as this one may need to be back buttered to get full coverage.

Clean out the excess thinset. A margin trowel is a perfect tool for removing thinset that has oozed into the grout joint. If grout doesn't get all the way into the joint, the resulting bond will be weak.

Does a Tile Look Off? Take It Out and Reset It

A day after setting the tile in this bathroom floor, I returned to apply the grout—and staring me right in the face was the corner of one tile that had sunk below its neighbors. Although the toilet would have camouflaged the problem, it was better to fix it before going any further.

Pulling a tile is not a big deal, providing you get to it before the thinset adhesive has had a chance to cure fully. In this case, the acrylic-modified thinset had been applied the previous afternoon, and it was still green. Using a hammer and a steel bar, I was able to jar the tile loose without too much trouble and without breaking the tile.

After scraping the semicured thinset off the back of the tile and the floor, I applied fresh thinset to both surfaces and rebedded the tile. This time, I was careful to keep the tile flush with those around it. This repair didn't take more than a few minutes, and as soon as the tile was reset, I grouted the entire floor. You never would have known anything was amiss.

When applying the thinset to the backer board for the tile, use the notched side and hold the trowel at 45 degrees to the floor so that an even amount of adhesive is applied and no air is trapped (see the bottom left photo on the facing page). What you want is 100 percent coverage of both the backer board and the back of the tile, with about ³⁄₃₂ in. of thinset between the two surfaces. Large tiles may have uneven backs, which will require you to back butter the surface with the flat side of a trowel.

Place the tile on the thinset with a slight twisting movement to help embed the tile fully (see the top right photo on the facing page). It's also a good idea to pull a tile off the floor near the start of the job to make sure you're using enough thinset. If the back of the tile is not fully covered, you'll know to adjust your technique or trowel or both (see the center right photo on the facing page), assuming the thinset has been mixed properly. Look on the label of the thinset bag for the proper notch size.

If, after a while, the thinset becomes too stiff or if tile doesn't readily stick to it, throw it away and mix a fresh batch. Before the thinset dries completely, you should clean the excess from the joints (see the bottom right photo on the facing page). If you don't, the grout may be too thin or will hydrate unevenly—two conditions that make a weak grout line.

Grout mix should be stiff. Holding a grout trowel at a 45-degree angle, the author works a stiff grout mix into joints between tiles. Excess grout should be troweled off as you go.

For a High-Strength Job, Don't Overwater the Grout

Grouting can make or break the tile job. A common mistake is adding too much water or admix when mixing the grout, which causes discoloration and a weaker mix. Another is using too much water when cleaning excess grout off the tile, which also can cause it to discolor. A third common error is using a high-speed mixer for the grout, which traps air in it and makes it weak.

Add only enough water to the grout powder to make it workable. Follow the manufacturer's recommended ratio of water to grout. Ideally, the grout should be a little

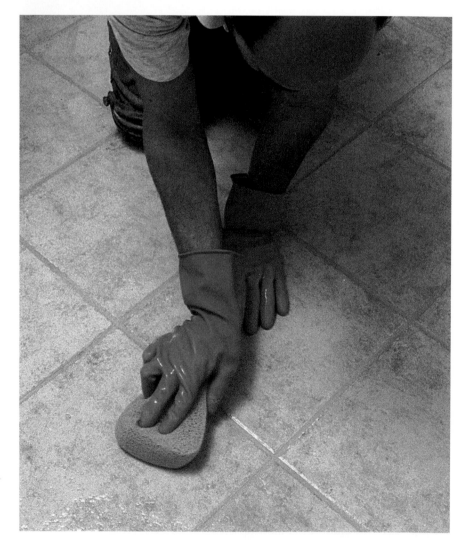

When a film appears, start cleaning. Not long after grout has been applied, a hazy film appears on the tile. That's a signal to start wiping the floor with a clean, damp sponge. Keep the pressure light.

Sources

**Tile Council
of America**
864-646-1787
www.tileusa.com

**James Hardie®
Interior Products**
1-888-JHARDIE
HardiBacker

This sponge needs a dunk. After a single light pass across the floor, this sponge has picked up plenty of excess grout. The author flips the sponge over, makes another light pass and then rinses out the sponge.

difficult to spread into the joints. If you're not going to mix the grout by hand, use a mixing paddle (the same type you would use for mixing thinset) and a slow-speed drill. After mixing, allow the grout to slake for 15 minutes and then remix it. At this point, you may add liquid or powder to adjust the consistency. As you work, remixing the grout occasionally will help keep it workable, but do not add more liquid.

Use a rubber grout trowel to spread the grout diagonally, holding the trowel at a 45-degree angle (see the top photo on the facing page). Grout King makes the best grout trowel I know, for about $13*, and they're available at most home centers or tile-supply stores. It's worth buying one even if you use it only once.

With all the joints filled and excess grout removed with the trowel, let the grout sit until it begins to firm and you see a dry film on the tile. Then it's time to begin cleaning the tile. You'll need at least two good hydro sponges (sold at tile-supply stores) and a large bucket of clean, cool water. After wetting and wringing out the sponge, wipe the surface to get even grout joints. Then, with a rinsed sponge, use one side of the sponge for one wipe in a diagonal direction (see the bottom photo on the facing page). After using both sides of the sponge, rinse it out (see the photo above). Change the water frequently to avoid spreading dirty water on the tile. You may have to make several passes to remove all the residue.

After the floor dries, you will see a film on the tile surface. This film can be polished off, but wait a bit until the grout is firmly set.

Price estimates noted are from 1999.

Dennis Hourany *owns Elite Tile in Walnut Creek, California.*

Installing a Leakproof Shower Pan

■ BY TOM MEEHAN

In the past 10 years, I have installed well over a thousand shower pans. Of all those pans, only two have leaked. One pan belonged to my father-in-law, and the other belonged to my dentist. My father-in-law is a conservative man who likes to have all his ducks in a row. My dentist was well aware that I had two root canals coming up in the near future. Needless to say, I made sure that fixing these two jobs moved to the top of my list.

After a lot of work, I found that faulty drain-assembly fittings were responsible for the leaks in both cases (honest). In the process of rebuilding the pans, I discovered a simple test (see the photo at left) that would have saved me all that misery. But more on that later; first, let's start building the pan.

The ultimate test. After the membrane is installed, the author plugs the drain and pours gallons of water into the shower. Better to find leaks now than after the tile is in.

Layers of a Shower Pan

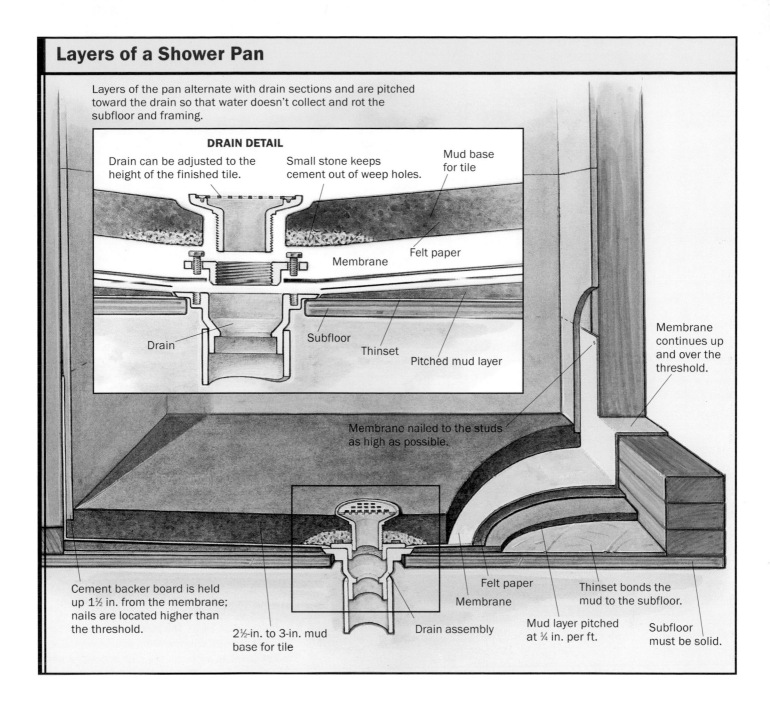

Layers of the pan alternate with drain sections and are pitched toward the drain so that water doesn't collect and rot the subfloor and framing.

DRAIN DETAIL

Drain can be adjusted to the height of the finished tile.

Small stone keeps cement out of weep holes.

Mud base for tile

Felt paper

Membrane

Drain

Subfloor

Thinset

Pitched mud layer

Membrane continues up and over the threshold.

Membrane nailed to the studs as high as possible.

Cement backer board is held up 1½ in. from the membrane; nails are located higher than the threshold.

2½-in. to 3-in. mud base for tile

Drain assembly

Felt paper

Membrane

Thinset bonds the mud to the subfloor.

Mud layer pitched at ¼ in. per ft.

Subfloor must be solid.

Pitch the Floor under the Membrane

Before I install the pan, I clean the subfloor in the shower area thoroughly. I look for anything that might punch or wear a hole in the membrane in the future. I set any nail heads in the lower 6 in. to 8 in. of the framing, and I put an extra flap of membrane over any nail plate installed to protect the plumbing.

When I'm building a shower pan, my first concern is that the subfloor is structurally sound. If it's not, I add a layer of ½-in. plywood before the plumber sets the drain assembly. I also do an extra step that I think makes a huge improvement over a standard installation. I like to pitch the shower floor to the drain area before I put the membrane material down (see the drawing above). A pitched mud base allows any water that may reach the membrane to drain through the weep holes in the drain assembly.

Thinset begins the shower pan. After the subfloor has been swept clean, a layer of latex-modified thinset is applied to bond the layer of mud that follows.

Getting the right slant. To build up the pitch on the pan floor, a fairly dry mix of 1 part portland cement to 3 parts or 4 parts sand is used to form the mud base. The mix should be just wet enough to form clumps when squeezed. Using a 2-ft. level as a gauge, the author floats a pitch of about ¼ in. per ft. from the pan's perimeter to the drain.

To create this pitch, I float a layer of mud over the shower floor. The mud, a mixture of 1 part portland cement to 3 parts or 4 parts sand, is just wet enough that it holds together if you grab a handful. To bond the mud layer to the plywood subfloor, I first apply a layer of latex-modified thinset to the subfloor (see the top left photo).

The mud mix is spread on top of the thinset, leaving a pitch of ¼ in. per ft. from the outside perimeter of the shower to the drain (see the photos at left and above). I pack the mud with a wooden float and smooth it with a flat steel trowel. This mud layer dries overnight.

The next day, I cover the mud with a layer of 15-lb. felt paper, cutting the paper tightly around the drain. The felt paper protects the membrane from any mud grit that could abrade it. The felt paper also isolates the finished shower pan from any movement that might occur in the subfloor.

A Vinyl Membrane Keeps the Water in the Pan

Now I'm ready for the shower-pan membrane. I use a vinyl membrane called Chloraloy® (see "Sources" on p. 47). I usually buy a 4-ft. by 50-ft. roll, which costs about $360. The membrane is also available by the piece; a 4-ft. by 6-ft. section costs about $50.

Map the Membrane

The membrane is rolled out on a clean floor, and the outer perimeter of the shower pan is drawn with a felt-tip pen and labeled as fold lines. An extra 7 in. is added in each direction, and the membrane is cut to those lines (see the left photo below). Once the membrane is centered in the shower, the excess is carefully folded into the corners (see the top right photo below). A roofing nail secures the fold to the framing (see the bottom right photo below). As the rest of the perimeter is tacked to the studs, the membrane should not be stretched too tightly.

I roll out the membrane on a clean floor and map out the pan with a felt-tip pen (see the left photo on p. 43). First, I draw the four sides of the shower pan (my fold lines) and then add 7 in. to each side for the cutlines. The fold lines let me position the membrane in the shower without having to shift it around a lot. Measuring and mapping the pan also help me avoid mistakes in my calculations. I always double-check the lines before cutting.

Folded Corners Let the Membrane Lie Flat

Before I move the membrane, I take off the top plastic ring of the drain assembly and put it aside until later. The bolts are left threaded into the lower drain assembly. I then drop the membrane into place, pushing all the fold lines to their proper outside edges.

In the corners where excess membrane bunches up, I push the liner directly into the corner with my finger. The excess corner material is then folded into a pleat so that it lies against the framing as flat as possible (see the top right photo on p. 43). Keeping the folds flat prevents bulges in the backer board, which is applied over the membrane.

I secure the fold to the framing with one roofing nail along the top edge (see the bottom right photo on p. 43). As I move toward the next corner, I nail the upper edge of the liner at each stud, always keeping the liner square to the wall and taking care not to pull it off the floor or to stretch it too tight.

One of the most crucial steps is cutting and connecting the membrane to the plastic drain assembly. First, I mark the heads of the four drain-assembly bolts where they touch the membrane (see the top left photo on the facing page). Then, with a fresh blade in my utility knife, I make a small slit for each bolt and push the membrane down over the bolts. Next, I cut from bolt to bolt in a circle following the inside of the drain

(see the top right photo on the facing page). Cuts should always be made toward the inside of the drain to avoid slipping with the knife and cutting the floor area of the membrane.

Before I install the top ring of the drain assembly, I lift the liner around the drain and make sure the bottom plastic ring is clear of dirt or grit. I like to adhere the underside of the membrane to the top of the drain-assembly plate with PVC membrane cement or an elastomeric sealant (see the bottom left photo on the facing page).

After applying the cement to both the membrane's underside and the top of the baseplate, I quickly press them together, place the top ring in position and slowly tighten the bolts, applying equal pressure on each bolt (see the bottom right photo on the facing page). At the threshold, I cut the membrane along the framed opening, fold it over and nail it to the threshold framing. To avoid leaks at the cut corners, I fold and glue additional pieces of membrane into the corners with PVC cement.

To test the pan, I first insert an expandable rubber drain plug into the lower part of the drain and tighten it with a wrench. I then dump enough water to cover the entire shower pan 2-in. to 3-in. deep (see the photo on p. 40), and I let the pan sit overnight. The next day, I make sure the level of the water hasn't gone down and then check for leaks in the ceiling directly below the shower stall.

I try to make it a point to have the builder or homeowner witness the shower-stall test. Once the pan has passed inspection, I make sure that no one steps into the shower pan until I have poured the mud base for the tile.

Cut Carefully to Connect the Drain

The drain must be assembled so that it forms a watertight seal with the membrane, so membrane cuts must be precise. First, bolt heads are marked (see the top left photo below). Next, small cuts are made to expose just the heads. Following the inside of the drain, a circular cut is made between bolt heads (see the top right photo below). After the membrane is cut, membrane adhesive or sealant is applied to the underside of the membrane (see the bottom left photo below). The top part of the drain is then slid into place and cemented, and bolts are tightened slowly and evenly (see the bottom right photo below).

Mark the bolt locations.

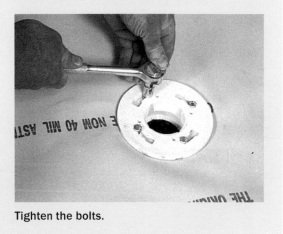

Cut in a circle between the bolts.

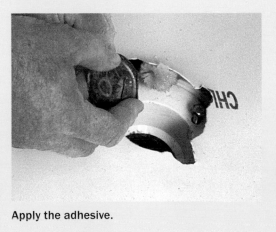

Apply the adhesive.

Tighten the bolts.

Keep the Backer Board up from the Shower Floor

All the shower stalls that I tile now have cement backer board under the wall tile. The bottom course of backer board is installed over the membrane, but I always try to install the upper sheets and the ceiling before the pan goes in to keep big clunky feet like mine off the delicate membrane. After the pan has been installed and tested, I put a protective layer of felt paper over the membrane while I hang the bottom pieces of backer board. All the backer board is attached to the studs with either 1½-in. galvanized roofing nails or galvanized screws. I make sure that the bottom pieces are at least

2 ft. wide to provide adequate strength for spanning the stud bays.

When installing the bottom course of backer board, I keep in mind two important rules. First, I keep the board 1½ in. from the pan floor. If the backer board is installed too low, moisture can wick up into the wall, creating a variety of problems. The second rule is never nail the board lower than the top of the threshold or the step into the shower. Nailing 4 in. from the finished floor usually works well. If the drain ever clogs, low nailing could cause a leak.

Thick Mud Makes a Sturdy Tile Base

I'm now ready to put the mud layer on top of the membrane. For this layer, I use a 4:1 mixture (sand to portland cement). I pour a couple of handfuls of ¼-in. stone around the base of the drain to help keep the weep holes in the drain assembly free and clear of cement (see the photo at left below).

Again, I mix the cement to a consistency that forms a ball when compressed in my hand (see the photo at right below). When I'm satisfied with the mix, I dump a good amount into the pan. The weight of the mix

Pitch the Second Mud Layer Smoothly to the Drain

A couple of handfuls of pea stone (see the left photo below) keeps the mud mix from clogging the weep holes in the drain. The mud for the shower floor should be just wet enough to stay in a clump when squeezed in the hand (see the right photo below). A 2-ft. level is used to make sure that the shower floor is flat and evenly pitched to the drain (see the top photo on the facing page). It does, however, double as the right tool for screeding the mud. The author rounds the corners of his steel trowel so that there are no sharp corners to puncture the membrane while he's working the mud layer (see the bottom photo on the facing page).

keeps the membrane from creeping. With this shower stall, I packed the cement about 2 in. to 3 in. thick to maintain the ¼-in.-per-ft. pitch from the wall to the drain that had already been established.

I used a 2-ft. level to straighten the perimeter of the mud layer. It's a good idea for beginners to establish a level line around the pan first. Again, I use a wooden float to pack the mud. A straightedge, in this case my 2-ft. level, and a flat steel trowel let me pitch the mud smoothly and evenly to the drain (see the top photo below). The upper portion of the drain can be adjusted so that it will be flush with the installed tile.

One precaution I take is to round over the corners of the steel trowel (see the bottom photo below). A square corner could slice or puncture the membrane if I'm not careful. I keep working the surface to eliminate any voids or low spots in the mud that can collect water once the tile is installed. When the mud layer is smooth, evenly pitched and level around the perimeter, I let it sit overnight, and then I'm ready to install the tile in the morning.

Tom Meehan *is a second-generation tile installer, owner of Cape Cod Tileworks in Harwich, Massachusetts, and co-author of* Build Like a Pro® Working with Tile *(The Taunton Press, Inc., 2005).*

Sources

The Noble Co.
800-878-5788
Chloraloy

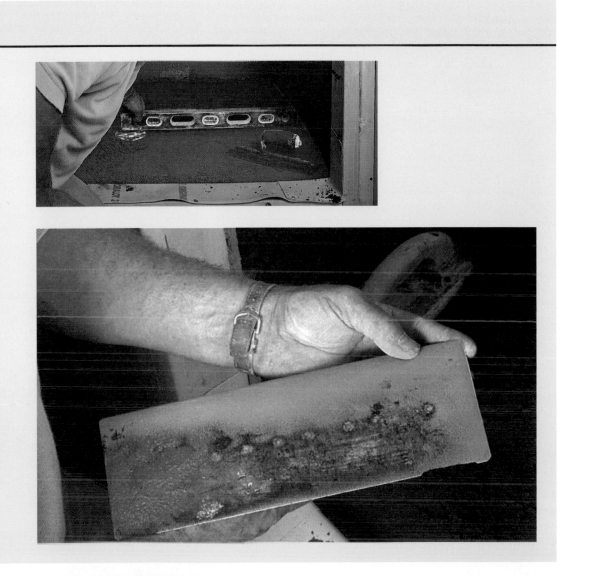

Details from Great Bathrooms

Natural light in the shower stall comes from above. A skylight over the shower sheds light on this extra-wide shower stall and tub. The limestone-tiled bench is a good shelf for plants or a seat for weary bathers.

Bright as a tropical bird. In their courtyard hacienda, architects Steven and Cathi House used color and light to their best advantages. Here, glass block in the bath wall lights the alcove, and small glass accents add bright spots to the black floor tile.

Materials accent a more subtle layout. Traditional at first glance, this bath has an elliptical wall built to follow the curve of the tub. The floor, shower and tub surround are Durango limestone; the vanity and moldings are clear maple.

Wide-open spaces of the western bath. Sharon Alber Fannin of Paradise Valley, Ariz., designed this bath with French doors that lead to a private courtyard. The glass shower enclosure offers counterpoint to the stained-stucco walls, tile and stone.

Broken-tile mosaic forms the centerpiece of the bath. Pink stucco and variegated floor tile surround a black porcelain toilet in this house in Mexico. A triptych of narrow windows overlooks the courtyard.

Water welling up from the rocks. Designed by Barry Gehl of Seattle, a carved basalt boulder serves as spigot and ladle bucket for this bluestone-bordered bathtub.

Clean lines for storage. Tempered-glass shelves make good use of wall space in a small bath, especially where there's little room for a linen closet.

Bathing in a sea of tile. In San Miguel de Allende, Mexico, Diane Kushner took advantage of the region's bounty of tile-makers and designed a colorful, tile-intensive bath.

The shower head hangs from the ceiling. A serpentine wall of glass block wraps this bath in Santa Monica, Calif. At the center, a Jacuzzi tub doubles as a shower.

Putting Tile to Work in the Kitchen

■ BY LANE MEEHAN

Our black Lab, Bogey, is a walking mud factory and sheds so much that he should be bald. When it came time to choose tile for our kitchen floor, we looked for tile that would help disguise evidence of Bogey and our three active boys. We chose a tile that looks like stone but in a color and finish that could hide dirt and dog hair until I had a spare moment to run the vacuum.

Our choice was based primarily on ease of maintenance, just one consideration when choosing kitchen tile. As a tile-store owner with a background in design, I field questions all the time about incorporating tile into clients' kitchens. This chapter addresses the questions I am asked most frequently.

What Types of Tile Can I Choose From?

The two most basic categories of tile are stone and ceramic. Stone tile is a natural product, mined or quarried directly from the earth. The three most common stones used

for tile are granite, marble and limestone, granite being the hardest.

Stone in its natural state is porous, so wherever it's used in a kitchen, it must be sealed to resist staining and discoloration. Stone tile has color all the way through, so deep scratches won't expose a different base color. However, a highly polished surface on a stone tile seems to accentuate even the smallest scratches. Stone can be installed on floors, countertops or backsplashes; however, it does tend to be a high-maintenance product.

On the other hand, ceramic tile is made from clay rolled flat and either sun-baked or fired in a kiln. There are hundreds of different clays, each with its own characteristics that can vary the tile's performance. Color is applied to ceramic tile in the form of baked-on glazes that also seal the tile.

In the past, ceramic-tile finishes had problems standing up to heavy use and abuse, but with recent technical advances, ceramic tile now performs better than it used to. With most ceramic tile, the color is

Tile outlines and defines kitchen
spaces. A tile border gives the island in
this kitchen, designed by Tim Quigley of
Minneapolis, its own separate visual
space. The backsplash behind the stove
forms a functional accent.

just on the surface, so deep scratches expose the clay below.

Porcelain is another manmade tile product. Porcelain is much denser than ordinary ceramic, making it harder to scratch and break. But as with stone, the shinier the surface of ceramic or porcelain, the more scratches will show. So I try not to use high-gloss tiles anywhere in a kitchen except on backsplashes, areas that are less susceptible to scratching. In the past, porcelain has been more expensive than ceramic, but improvements in technology have reduced the price.

Beyond the amount of gloss, tile finishes can vary greatly. Tile finishes are graded by their ability to resist wear due to traffic; a light-industrial tile has a higher durability rating than most residential-grade tiles. Industrial-rated tile is a bit more expensive, but the extra cost makes sense if your kitchen resembles a freeway. In addition to a durability rating, the Tile Council of America (see "Sources" on p. 59) gives tile a coefficient of friction (COF) rating, which indicates how slippery the surface will be underfoot. But if the tile feels too smooth or too slick to the touch, it will probably be too slippery to use on the floor.

How Do Lifestyle and Lighting Affect Choices?

The first thing I ask clients about is their family, their lifestyle and the way their kitchen is going to be used. For example, for a client who has a large family or who does a lot of entertaining, the kitchen is a busy hub with a casual atmosphere. For this kitchen, I might suggest warm-colored tile with perhaps a softer stone look.

After the client's lifestyle, I look at the type of lighting in the kitchen. If it is blessed with a great deal of natural light from windows or skylights, tumbled marble tile or tile with a matte finish will absorb light and create a softer look (see the photo

Multipurpose porcelain

Ceramic wall tile with blue crackle glaze

Commercial ceramic wall tile

Rosso-Verona tumbled marble

Handmade glazed wall tile

Handmade sanded floor tile

Porcelain floor tile

Limestone tile

Stone look-alike ceramic tile

Marble floor or wall tile

on the facing page). A textured surface on the tile softens the effect even further.

On the other hand, tile with a glossy finish reflects light and helps brighten areas of a kitchen that are dimly lighted or that receive little or no natural light. Remember

Tile can act as a dimmer switch. This kitchen gets lots of light from two sides. The natural colors and matte finish of the tumbled-marble countertop and backsplash help soften the light and cut down on glare in a kitchen with a lot of windows.

that glossy tile used in a kitchen with a lot of light, either natural or artificial, requires more frequent cleaning because fingerprints and water spots tend to show up more.

When choosing tile, I also look at the color and finish of the cabinets and countertops. If the counters and cabinets have a matte or satin finish, then I try to keep the same feel in the floors and the backsplash. By the same token, if the kitchen has the polished, streamlined look of many contemporary kitchens, I suggest a straightforward tile pattern with a glossy finish.

Tile color can make a large contribution toward a warm or cool feel in a kitchen. The earthy tones of limestone or tumbled marble are the warmest of the tile colors, while bright whites and blues tend to be quite cool. But even cool colors can be warmed with colored grout. For example, an ivory or off-white grout color can take the cool edge off bright white. The reverse can be true if you're trying to achieve a formal or industrial feel with gray or blue tile. A steel-gray grout helps create a crisp, cool look.

Will My Three Boys and the Family Dog Hurt My Tile Floor?

A client's lifestyle has the biggest bearing on the choice of floor tile. If you'd rather spend time with your three growing boys than take care of your kitchen floor, I suggest tile that hides a multitude of sins (and dirt) and always seems to look nice, such as a ceramic-stone look-alike (see the photo on p. 56). A quick vacuum and an occasional mopping, and you're off and running.

If cooking and entertaining are big parts of your life, then I'd suggest tile that won't stain if hot grease and oil or an occasional glass of wine is spilled on it. A glazed ceramic tile works best in this situation, but for an Old World look, you can use a real stone, such as limestone. If you select a stone tile

No time for cleaning? For busy, active families with kids and pets, consider a tile floor with a lot of color variations such as this stone look-alike. It stays better looking longer between cleanings.

floor, be sure to treat it with a good sealer according to the manufacturer's directions. We recommend either Miracle Sealants Porous Plus or One Master Marble and Stone Care's Gold Shield (see "Sources") for sealing stone tile.

No matter what tile you choose for your kitchen floor, the grout should also be sealed. To make the grout more impervious to spills and stains, I recommend starting with a latex-modified grout or one that is mixed with a latex additive instead of water. Once the grout has cured properly, a sealer such as Miracle Sealants Porous Plus will fight off most food incursions.

Another grout option is epoxy, which is stain resistant and does not require sealing. But because epoxy is harder to work with for the installer, we generally use it for smaller areas, such as countertops. With some tile, such as limestone, epoxy grout is not recommended, so be sure to check with manufacturers' suggestions.

How Does a Tile Floor Relate to Adjacent Rooms?

The kitchen-floor tile should help establish a visual flow into the surrounding areas, so I ask clients about the colors and materials on the floors of the rooms that are adjoining the kitchen. For example, if the kitchen floor joins up with a dark wood floor in the dining room, consider using tile with a warm, medium color to cut down on the visual contrast between rooms. If the kitchen floor meets colored carpet in an adjacent room, keep in mind that you'll probably change the carpet at some point, so choose a neutral tile color that will go with future carpet choices.

Tile thickness is another consideration. Whether the kitchen floor butts up against other existing tile, hardwood floors or carpet, the tile installer will need to install some sort of threshold to create a clean transition into the next room. Tile thickness can also affect doors that swing into the kitchen, as well as appliances, such as dishwashers or trash compactors, that have to fit under the countertops in a kitchen.

Can Tile Make My Tiny Kitchen Look Bigger?

Tile layout can have a big impact on a room's appearance. While a parallel or straight pattern can intensify the narrowness of a kitchen, a diagonal tile pattern makes a room look wider (see the drawings on the facing page).

Tile size can also affect the appearance of the room. The smaller the tile, the busier the grout–joint pattern. The simple grout–joint pattern you get with larger 10-in. to 12-in. tiles can make a small room look larger. Smaller 4-in. to 6-in. tiles on a floor can have the opposite effect, creating a mosaic pattern or a cobblestone look.

Clipping the corners of square tiles creates hexagons or octagons with small square spaces left between. The small tiles (called dots) that fill the spaces can introduce a dash of color to the floor in a pattern that breaks up the simple straight lines.

Irregular tile patterns such as block random (using three sizes of tile) or a pinwheel

Tile Patterns at Work

The right pattern can make a kitchen look wider. Floor tile installed in a straight pattern makes a narrow room seem narrower (see the near right drawing) while tile in a diagonal pattern softens the tunnel effect of a long, narrow kitchen, making it seem wider (see the far right drawing).

pattern can help unify a kitchen that has many entrances and exits. These patterns also work well to blend together tile that is highly varied in color. A tile border on the floor can make a kitchen look cozier by bringing the eye in or by creating a frame around the kitchen table or an island (see the photo on p. 53).

Is Tile OK for a Kitchen Countertop?

Granite-slab countertops have long been popular in high-end kitchens. Tile countertops, both ceramic and stone, have some of the same attributes as slabs, such as durability and heat resistance, but at less than half the cost, depending on the tile you choose.

Granite tile can be installed with tight grout joints to give the impression of a solid slab. And with granite tile, it's easy to add a border to accent or complement the color of the stone. One drawback to stone tile on a countertop is the edges. Although you can round over the edges, granite tile is thinner than a solid slab (⅜ in. to ½ in. compared with 1¼ in., normal thickness for a granite slab), so it's tougher to get the same full-slab

look. Another drawback is not being able to install an undermount sink with granite tile.

Although the tight grout joints of granite tile create a good, smooth work surface, machine-made ceramic tile with standard grout joints makes a slightly rougher work surface.

Handmade tile is usually installed with wider grout joints that are charming, but its inherently bumpy surface can be difficult to work on and can cause wineglasses and bowls to tip over (see the photos on p. 58).

The edges of a tile countertop can be addressed in various ways. Continuing the tile over the edge gives the countertop a thick look. Relief tile, such as a rope pattern, can turn countertop edges into a visual focal point. Wooden edges that match or complement cabinets are also popular (see the top photo on p. 58).

As on floors, borders on countertops can add decoration. But if it's used in too large an area or if a lot of items are stored on the counter, a border can be lost or distracting.

Tile can also be combined with other types of surfaces for a dramatic look (see the photo on p. 55). For instance, the savings from tiling most of the countertop might

Handmade tile is pretty but uneven. The irregular surface of handmade ceramic tile is a challenge to work on and can be hazardous to wineglasses. Cutting boards should always be used on tile countertops.

as granite or marble, can lose their shine when exposed to some food acids.

As in floors, latex-modified grout should be used on tiled countertops along with a good coat of grout sealer. Again, epoxy grout, which costs a little more and is a little harder to install, will make the grout impenetrable.

Should the Backsplash Blend or Make a Splash?

A tile backsplash is the spot where you can be really creative with tile in the kitchen (see the right photo on the facing page). Because a backsplash functions to protect the wall from splashes and splatters that come from cooking and preparing food, the only prerequisite is that backsplash tile be easy to keep clean. Beyond that, the choices become mainly aesthetic.

I always ask clients how much stuff they plan to keep on their countertops. Toasters, microwaves and canisters tend to block the backsplash, and in that case, the backsplash just provides a backdrop of color and texture. I usually recommend extending the tile from the countertop all the way to the bottoms of the wall cabinets so that the backsplash acts as a visual connection between the upper and lower cabinets.

Borders usually work best above long stretches of counter that are uninterrupted by windows or appliances. And when installed three-quarters of the way up the backsplash, a border won't get lost near the countertop or under the wall cabinets. At that height, a border will usually clear the height of the toaster or a bowl of fruit for a continuous line.

If the client is thinking of having decorative tiles scattered randomly throughout the backsplash, I suggest taping playing cards to the wall at random to see if the effect works in that particular kitchen. Playing cards can also be used in a line to test the visual power of a border.

leave enough money for a solid slab of granite in the sink area for an undermount sink. A stone slab or a wood surface on only the island could make a bold statement while providing a smooth surface for an informal eating area.

Can Tile Be Used as a Cutting Board?

Although few tile or stone surfaces can stand up to a sharp kitchen knife, most hold up well under other kitchen rigors such as abuse from pots and pans. Limestone scratches easily, but those scratches can be sanded out. Surfaces such as glossy tile or highly polished granite tend to show marks more readily, and their scratches are harder to remove or cover up. Stone or ceramic tile with a matte finish tends to hide scratches and surface abrasions better.

Stone tile is also porous, so it has to be sealed properly to resist staining from things such as red wine and grease. And some ceramic tiles, as well as polished stone such

Isn't Tile Expensive?

Tile varies greatly in price, and budget is a concern for the vast majority of my clients. So here's my strategy for keeping costs down. First, use reasonably priced machine-made tile for large areas in the kitchen. Then there will be money left for those handmade borders, small murals or strategically placed accent tiles that will give your kitchen a rich look without breaking the bank (see the left photo below).

Installation prices can vary greatly depending on the type of tile, the layout and the conditions of the existing floors and walls. A tile installer can explain what your options are and how much each option costs. Even if you opt for a less expensive installation, always seal the tile. Sealing tile is pretty easy, so you can save a little by doing it yourself. Spend some money on a good sealer.

For good ceramic floor tile, expect to pay between $2.85* and $5.50/sq. ft. Above $5.50/sq. ft., the market really explodes, and there is a huge range of floor tiles to choose from. Wall tiles start at around $2.50/sq. ft. Installation prices vary around the country, but here on Cape Cod, installing ceramic tile costs $4 to $5/sq. ft. on top of the price of the tile.

Price estimates noted are from 1999.

---

*When she's not taking her three sons to karate practice, **Lane Meehan** and her husband, Tom, own and manage Cape Cod Tileworks in Harwich, Massachusetts. She is the co-author of* Build Like a Pro® Working With Tile *(The Taunton Press, Inc., 2005).*

Sources

Tile Council of America
864-646-8453
www.tileusa.com

Miracle Sealants Company
12318 Lower Azusa Rd.
Arcadia, CA 91006
800-350-1901
www.miraclesealants.com
Porous Plus

One Master Marble and Stone Care
800-254-7166
www.prosoco.com
Gold Shield

Tile Art and Accents

The backsplash of cows in a pasture (right) in this kitchen designed by Randy Fritz of Lakeside, Calif., combines the art of Roger Dunham of Petaluma, Calif., with the practicality of ceramic tile. Random decorative tiles in a backsplash of less expensive, machine-made tile (below) give this kitchen a colorful accent.

Tiling a Kitchen Counter

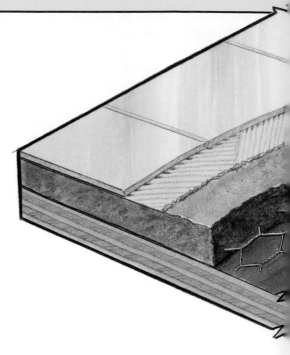

■ BY DENNIS HOURANY

It took two days to complete my first shower, including the time I spent at the library reading up on how to do it. That was 26 years ago. Since then, I've laid hundreds of tile floors and counters. My San Francisco-area tile contracting company often works in housing developments, where a journeyman tilesetter with only one helper can set a tile counter in a single day. Even if you don't set as much tile as we do, installing a kitchen counter should be a straightforward and relatively speedy process.

Tile can be set on either a mortar bed or cement board (see the photos below). Around here, counters are almost always set on a mortar bed ¾ in. thick. I think that produces the best tile job—it's strong, durable and easily leveled. Whichever substrate you choose, the processes of laying out the counter and installing the tile are identical.

Before you put down either cement board or a mortar bed, make sure you have a solid wood base on top of the cabinets. I use a ¾-in., exterior-grade plywood (although you can also use 1x6 boards with ¼-in. gaps

DON'T GET HUNG UP ON THE SUBSTRATE
Dennis Hourany starts a tiled kitchen counter with a mortar bed (see the left photo below), but you don't have to. Cement board (see the right photo below) is another choice. For more on cement board, see "Cement Board Is a Quick Alternative to a Mortar Bed" on pp. 64–65.

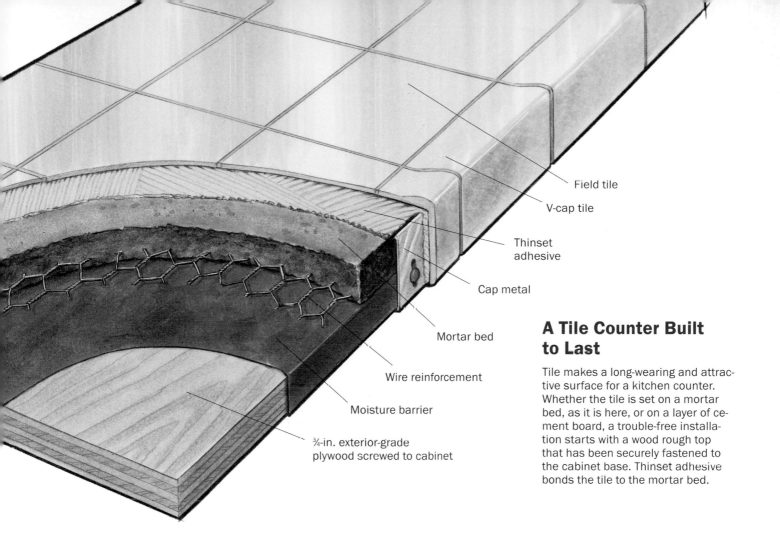

Field tile

V-cap tile

Thinset adhesive

Cap metal

Mortar bed

Wire reinforcement

Moisture barrier

¾-in. exterior-grade plywood screwed to cabinet

A Tile Counter Built to Last

Tile makes a long-wearing and attractive surface for a kitchen counter. Whether the tile is set on a mortar bed, as it is here, or on a layer of cement board, a trouble-free installation starts with a wood rough top that has been securely fastened to the cabinet base. Thinset adhesive bonds the tile to the mortar bed.

between them). If you use plywood, it's a good idea to make a series of cuts through the sheet with a circular saw to prevent the rough top from warping. Snap a series of parallel lines 6 in. to 8 in. apart along the length of the plywood, then make 6-in.- to 8-in.-long cuts along the lines, leaving 6 in. to 8 in. between them. Where overhangs are larger than about 8 in., you must provide adequate support—with corbels, for example—to prevent movement in the plywood that would crack the tile or grout.

Protect Cabinets from Moisture

Mortar is wet stuff, so we install a moisture barrier over the rough top of the cabinet. You may use an asphalt-impregnated paper, such as 30–30 kraft paper, 15-lb. roofing felt or 4-mil polyethylene film. When we staple

the material to the rough top, we let it hang all the way to the floor to protect the cabinets as we install tile. Excess paper can be trimmed away later. Paper should cover all rough-top edges, including those around the sink cutout and any other openings. Seams should be lapped at least 2 in. If you are installing backsplash tiles over a mortar bed, extend the paper up the wall beyond where the tile will end to protect the wall. Or use masking tape to protect untiled areas of the wall above the backsplash.

A mortar bed should be reinforced with some kind of metal lath. The kind approved by the Tile Council of America is a galvanized, expanded type that should weigh at least 2½ lb. per sq. yd. We use 1-in., 20-ga. galvanized stucco netting or chicken wire. I like to run the wire on the deck and up the wall to within ½ in. of where the tile will stop, provided the backsplash tile does not

Getting the kinks out. To avoid kinks in the cap metal where it goes around a curve in the counter's edge, make a series of cuts in the top edge at the bend with a pair of aviation snips.

Cap metal supports the mortar. Elite Tile's Ernie Grijalva loosely nails cap metal to the edge of a counter. Moisture-resistant, asphalt-impregnated kraft paper protects the plywood.

Level the metal. Once the cap metal has been leveled, Grijalva drives the nails home. By keeping the top edge of the cap metal ¾ in. above the top, he knows the counter will be thick enough at any point.

A second nail for insurance. Slots in the cap metal allow it to be adjusted up and down for level. Once leveled, the cap metal is anchored with a second nail driven right through the metal.

extend up the wall more than roughly 8 in. If your plan is to carry the tile all the way to the bottom of the upper cabinets, then cut the wire at the juncture between deck and backsplash and install a separate piece of wire on the wall.

We staple the wire every 4 in. to 6 in. with staples at least ⅜ in. long. After the wire comes cap metal, which supports the perimeter of the mortar bed and is used as a guide to screed the surface (see the center photo above). Cap metal comes in a variety of shapes and sizes. We typically finish counter edges with a piece of tile called V-cap, which forms a 90-degree tile corner, so our cap metal is usually the J-cap variety. You can get cap metal at tile-supply houses or at some of the super hardware stores.

One big advantage of a mortar bed is that you can provide a level surface for tile even if the cabinets are not quite level—something that's harder to do when you're using cement board. So make sure the top edge of the cap metal is level before you start snugging up the nails and fixing the cap in place (see the photos above).

Two Kinds of Mortar Make a Bed That Can Be Tiled the Same Day

We use two types of mortar in a counter: fat mud and deck mud. Because it contains lime, fat mud is sticky enough to adhere to vertical surfaces. For most horizontal surfaces, we use deck mud, a much drier mix that's not as susceptible to shrinking or cracking.

Fat mud (no, I'm not sure how it got its name) is a mixture of 5 parts plaster sand, 1 part portland cement and 1 part type-S or comparable lime. These three ingredients are mixed thoroughly before clean water is added. Consistency is crucial. If the mortar is too wet, it won't stay on the trowel. If it's too dry, it won't stick to the wall.

We mix a batch of this mortar first, but before applying any of it, we install wooden screed strips on vertical surfaces to determine the depth of the mud bed. Make the strips ½ in. thick and nail them right to the wall over the wire. We use 1½-in. drywall nails, which are easy to pull out later; avoid nailing the screed to a stud. Screed strips should be placed near edges and at intervals so that you will be able to span the distance between them with a straightedge.

We work fat mud firmly into the chicken wire on all vertical surfaces. This is called a scratch coat, and it's essential for getting the rest of the mortar bed to stay put. We bank

MIX TWO KINDS OF MORTAR

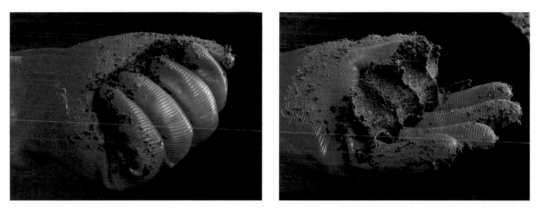

Deck mud is a dry mix. Add just enough water so that the mortar holds its shape when it is compressed into a ball.

Fat mud for edges and vertical surfaces. Grijalva's helper, Martin Arellano, builds a layer of fat mud along the edge of the sink cutout. The limed mortar sticks to surfaces and holds its shape.

With both types of mortar in place, Grijalva uses an aluminum straightedge to screed the countertop. One end rides on a piece of cap metal that has been leveled and tamped in the mortar.

Cement Board Is a Quick Alternative to a Mortar Bed

In Dennis Hourany's part of the country, the West Coast, a mortar bed is usually specified as the substrate for a tiled kitchen counter. But tilesetters in other regions may prefer a cement-board underlayment, such as Durock or WonderBoard® (see "Sources" on p. 70). These panels, made of portland cement and reinforcing fiberglass mesh, speed up preparation of the tile substrate considerably.

For Tom Meehan, a tilesetter in Harwich, Mass., cement board is the substrate of choice for kitchen counters (see the drawing below). It bonds well with the thinset adhesive used to set the tile, and it can be installed quickly.

Cement board is fairly easy to cut (see photos 1–3 on the facing page). Treat the material like drywall—score a line with a utility knife a few times, snap the board along the line and then cut the back of the board along the break. You can get a smoother cut with a circular saw and carbide blade, but be careful. Breathing the dust is unhealthy. Meehan suggests cutting the board outside and making sure you wear a respirator.

Before installing the cement board, Meehan screws down a layer of ¾-in. exterior-grade plywood on the top of the cabinet. Screw heads should be flush with the surface. Next is a layer of thinset mortar or construction adhesive (see photo 4 on the facing page), followed by ½-in.-thick cement board. If you're using construction adhesive, work quickly because it begins to skim over in about five minutes and loses its pliability.

Meehan presses the cement board into place and jiggles it gently to even out the adhesive beneath it. The cement board is attached with 1¼-in. galvanized drywall screws 8 in. on center (see photo 5 on the facing page). You may want to drill pilot holes.

If kitchen cabinets already have laminate counters that are structurally sound, you can leave them in place and put down ¼-in. or ⁵⁄₁₆-in. cement board right on top of the laminate. Laminate should be scuffed with a 50-grit sandpaper first. The total substrate should be no less than 1¼ in. thick.

Edges can be handled a couple of ways. In the installation featured here, Meehan brings the cement board flush to the edge of the plywood and then finishes the edge with a layer of thinset and fiberglass mesh tape (see photo 6 on the facing page). Another approach is to finish the outside edge with a vertical strip of cement board, and then apply a layer of thinset and mesh tape.

Cement board is available in thicknesses of ¼ in., ⁵⁄₁₆ in., ⁷⁄₁₆ in., ½ in. and ⅝ in. Sheets may be 32 in., 36 in. or 48 in. wide.

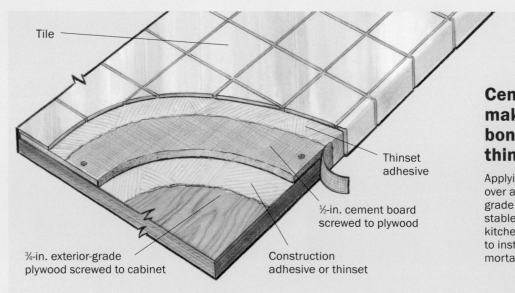

Tile

Thinset adhesive

½-in. cement board screwed to plywood

¾-in. exterior-grade plywood screwed to cabinet

Construction adhesive or thinset

Cement board makes a good bond with thinset adhesive

Applying ½-in. cement board over a layer of ¾-in. exterior-grade plywood makes a stable substrate for a tiled kitchen counter. It's faster to install than a traditional mortar bed.

1. **Score cement board with a knife.** Tilesetter Tom Meehan uses a utility knife and a straight-edge to score a piece of Durock cement board.

2. **Score the back, too.** After snapping the cement board along the score line, Meehan cuts through the back of the sheet, like working with dry wall.

5. **Screws hold the cement board down.** Galvanized drywall screws 8 in. o.c. keep the cement board in place while the adhesive sets up.

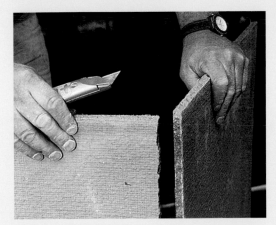

3. **The board should break cleanly.** Once fibers on the back of the board have been severed, the sheet should break cleanly along the score line.

4. **Bond the cement board to the counter.** A bead of construction adhesive may be used to bond the cement board to the rough top.

Although Meehan thinks cement board is best, another possibility is a material called DensShield® made by Georgia-Pacific (see "Sources"), which was recommended recently by a number of *Fine Homebuilding* readers on "Breaktime," the magazine's web discussion group (finehomebuilding.com). Georgia-Pacific says DensShield is one-third lighter than portland-cement backer board and is more water resistant than cement-board products. The company says the board has a proprietary heat-cured surface with a silicone-treated core embedded with glass mats.

6. **Finish edges with thinset.** Fiberglass mesh tape and a thin layer of thinset adhesive finish the edges. This substrate is now ready for tile.

Scott Gibson was a senior editor of Fine Homebuilding *and is the author of* The Workshop *(The Taunton Press, Inc., 2003).*

fat mud against all the cap metal along out-side edges, from the top of the metal down to the deck at about a 45-degree angle. Finally, fat mud is used around all deck penetrations, such as the sink cutout, because it holds its shape there better than deck mud (see the bottom left photo on p. 63).

After troweling a generous layer of fat mud on the backsplash area, we use a length of straight aluminum or wood to screed the surface and then fill any low spots and screed again. At this point, we remove the screed strips that were nailed to the wall and gently fill in the voids with mortar. Any excess may be cut away once the mortar has firmed up.

Deck mud is used to fill in the remainder of the countertop. It consists of 5 parts sand and 1 part portland cement. Mix these ingredients thoroughly before adding water—and remember to keep the mix dry (see the top left photo on p. 63). It should not ooze through your fingers. Trowel and pack down the deck mud over the deck to an elevation slightly higher than the cap metal.

We do not use wooden screeds on the countertop. Instead, we use a level to create several flat spots and then tamp in lengths of cap metal to guide the aluminum straightedge. Locations for these screed pads are somewhat strategic. They need to be placed at all turns in the counter as well as at intermediate locations to allow the straightedge to cover the entire countertop. The cap metal at the edges of the counter also acts as a screed.

Once you have spread enough mortar on the top, use a straightedge to screed off the excess (see the bottom right photo on p. 63), fill the low spots and screed again, then remove the cap-metal pieces used as screed pads. A wooden trowel will not bring water to the surface like a metal tool will, but one last pass with a flat-edged metal trowel leaves a smoother finish.

A Few Fundamentals Help Make Tile Layout Less Complicated

Laying out individual tiles so that the job is aesthetically pleasing as a whole is no easy feat, especially in those kitchens where counters wrap around corners or make angled jogs. It is virtually a given that tiles will have to be cut somewhere. The trick is in making the cuts where they are least obvious and making the tile pattern as a whole pleasing to the eye.

A few fundamentals will help. First, try to lay out the counter so that no tile you set is less than half its original size. Second, never break, or interrupt, grout lines unless you are using two different-size tiles or unless you can dramatically improve the layout by doing so. Grout lines generally should be continuous as they move from the counter-top to the backsplash or up other vertical surfaces. Although it's a matter of personal preference, I look at countertop penetrations, such as a cooktop or sink, as unavoidable interruptions in the tile job as a whole—not something the tile layout should be maneuvered around.

We begin setting tiles immediately after the mortar bed has been leveled and tamped. But first, we mark out reference lines along the edges of the counter to indicate where the V-cap starts (see the photos at left on the facing page).

I start with full tiles on as many of the leading or open edges of the counter as possible (see the drawing on the facing page). Open edges are those that do not abut a restraining edge, such as a wall or a raised counter. Cut tiles should go at the back. In many of the kitchens we do, L- and U-shaped counters are common, so we are careful to start the first full tile as shown in the drawing. This layout ensures the greatest number of full-field tiles and the fewest disruptions in the overall pattern.

TILE-LAYOUT BASICS

Ready for layout. With the mortar bed tamped and leveled, a piece of V-cap is used to set layout lines. Grijalva uses a utility knife to mark the inside edge.

Snap lines around the perimeter. After marking all counter edges with the V-cap, Grijalva and his helper snap chalklines. These control lines are essential for setting straight courses of field tile.

It would be impossible to cover all the layout problems you may have to wrestle with. For this reason, consider using a story pole, which you can make yourself. Lay tiles in a row on the floor with the desired grout spacing. Place a length of wood alongside these tiles, and mark it where tiles fall. You can place the story pole at any point on the area to be tiled and see right away what your cuts will look like. If you're tiling for someone other than yourself, it may be best to involve him or her in layout decisions, and a story pole can be a big help in explaining

Keep cut tiles at the back of the counter

In this counter of 6x6 tile, layout starts with control lines showing where field tiles end and V-cap starts. The first full tile is set at the intersection of two control lines. Where possible, cut tiles are kept at the back of the counter.

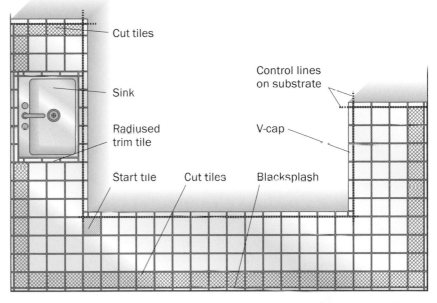

Cut tiles

Sink

Control lines on substrate

Radiused trim tile

V-cap

Start tile   Cut tiles   Blacksplash

Keep grout lines straight. When turning a corner, a framing square prevents wandering grout lines. If tile is being set over a mortar bed before it is cured, be careful not to mar the surface.

A straightedge makes diagonal cuts easier. Grijalva lays dry tile on the mortar bed, then marks the tile with a straightedge. After the tiles have been cut, thinset and tile are brought to the layout line.

the options. You also can simply lay out tiles to test a pattern, but a story pole is faster. You may find that starting the tile in a different spot yields the best overall countertop pattern with the fewest awkward cuts.

Sinks can be handled in several ways. One option is to set a self-rimming sink on top of the field tile once the counter is done.

INSIDE ANGLES CALL FOR MITERED EDGE PIECES

Use scrap to find the inside corner. Mitering the two pieces of V-cap meeting in this 45° corner will make the neatest job. To start, Grijalva uses two offcuts to establish the corner, then measures for the first mitered piece of V-cap.

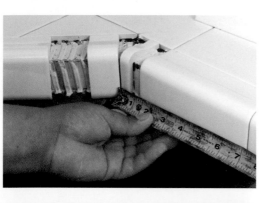

Eye the cut on a tile saw. By aligning one pencil mark on the slot in the saw's sliding table and the other mark with the blade, you can make an accurate miter cut on a tile saw.

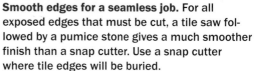

Smooth edges for a seamless job. For all exposed edges that must be cut, a tile saw followed by a pumice stone gives a much smoother finish than a snap cutter. Use a snap cutter where tile edges will be buried.

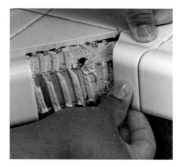

One down, one to go. This piece of mitered V-cap fits the space perfectly, but it's safer to dry-fit both pieces before applying any mastic.

Now fit the second piece. With the first mitered section in place, Grijalva can mark and cut the second piece of V-cap. The result is a neat, well-fitting corner.

For a neater appearance, set the sink in the mortar bed before field tile is laid, then use trim tiles with a radiused edge as a border.

Field Tiles Are Set in an Even Layer of Thinset Adhesive

The adhesive used to bond tile to either a mortar bed or cement board is called dry-set mortar or thinset. We use basic thinset on ceramic and other pervious tiles. Latex- or polymer-modified thinset is a good choice for impervious tile such as porcelain. Instructions printed on the bag will tell you which size notched trowel to use and how to apply the thinset. It is crucial to follow the instructions exactly. You should mix only enough thinset that can be tiled over within 15 minutes. Don't let it skim over.

The only spot where we don't use thinset is on the edges where V-cap tiles are installed. We have seen these tiles crack when thinset is used, possibly because the thinset makes a rigid bond that's tough on the 90-degree edge of the V-cap if there's any flex in the rough top. We now use premixed tile mastic for these edge pieces. Mastic stays more pliable than thinset, and the edge tiles don't crack.

Thinset should not ooze up more than two-thirds of the way into the grout joint. If that seems to be happening, you may be using a trowel with too deep a notch or you may not be applying a consistent amount of thinset. When you get too much thinset in a joint, simply rake it out.

We start with a full tile at the intersection of control lines on the countertop. Many tiles are produced with spacers, called lugs, on the edges. You can set the tiles together or space them farther apart, but never wider than the thickness of the tile so that the grout won't crack. To help keep the joints consistent if the spacing is greater than the lugs provide, you can use plastic spacers available where you buy tile.

But don't count on spacers to keep the lines straight—that is what control lines and straightedges are for. A framing square helps keep tiles aligned when turning corners (see the center photo on p. 67), and aluminum angle stock is invaluable for staying on track—we keep several different lengths on all our jobs. A good alternative is a straight piece of wood.

Some counter shapes require a number of tiles to be cut on a diagonal at the counter edge (see the right photo on p. 67). In these situations, we lay these tiles out dry (no thinset) so that they can be marked with a pencil and straightedge. Once the tiles are cut on a tile saw, the thinset can be troweled on and the tiles set in place. Inside corners and curved edges can be tricky, but they are easily managed with a little care (see the photos on the facing page).

A tile saw is indispensable. Rent one if you can't find a friend who will loan you one. A saw produces a clean cut that needs only a little touch up with a pumice stone. Snap cutters are faster, but the edge isn't smooth enough to be shown on the finished counter. We use snap cutters when the edge will be buried, such as at the back of the counter where the backsplash hides any roughness. And when you pick up your tile supplies, make sure you ask for plastic wedges and corner pieces (see "Special Pieces" at right).

Grouting Is the Final Step

Grouting is easy if you follow two simple rules. First, use the proper tools—a smooth, hard-rubber grout float and top-quality hydro sponges. Second, and most important, follow the grout manufacturer's instructions. Even the best tools can't salvage a job when the grout has been mixed or applied improperly. Tile adhesive should cure for at least 24 hours before grout is applied. Before getting started, remove any

SPECIAL PIECES

Don't forget these when you buy your tile. Specially shaped tile pieces make fast work of inside and outside corners.

Inside corner at top of backsplash

V-cap outside corner

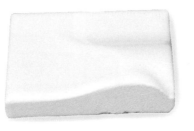
V-cap inside corner

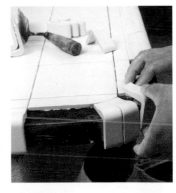

These will help, too. Plastic wedges sold by tile suppliers make it easy to get the top edge of the backsplash to line up perfectly.

RADIUSED CORNERS NEED SPECIAL FITTING

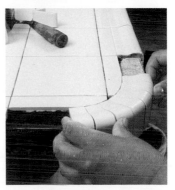

Rounding the bend. Grijalva pencils in the line where a field tile will have to be cut to fit a radiused corner. He cuts the curves on a tile saw by nibbling to the line. Pie-shaped pieces of V-cap, cut by eye and tested until they fit, complete the corner.

FINISHING UP

Wait a day before grouting.
Once the thinset has cured, mix grout to a creamy consistency and force the material into the gaps between tiles with a hard-rubber float. Work the float at an angle.

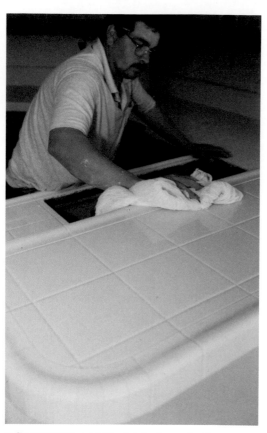

Keep the sponge clean. A tile sponge cleans up the residue. Be careful not to dig out any grout, and rinse the sponge frequently.

A final polish, and the job is done. Arellano uses a generous pad of clean cheesecloth to remove the haze left by the tile sponge. The surface polishes quickly.

Sources

United States Gypsum Co.
125 S. Franklin St.
Chicago, IL 60606
800-874-4968
www.usg.com
Durock

Custom Building Products
800-272-8786
www.custombuildingprojects.com
WonderBoard

Georgia-Pacific
800-284-5347
www.gp.com
DensShield

loose material from the joints. You also may want to apply a grout release to the surface of unglazed tiles to prevent staining.

Grout stays workable for about two hours. You should restir the grout mix periodically as you work, but do not add any more liquid to it. If the grout becomes too stiff to work, throw it out and make a fresh batch.

Once the grout is mixed and you've removed any debris from the joints, use the hard-rubber float to force grout into the joints (see the top left photo above). Work diagonally using enough pressure to ensure the joints are filled. Then remove excess grout with the edge of the float. After allowing the grout to set up for 15 minutes or so, wet and ring out a sponge and wipe the tile

diagonally (see the bottom left photo above).

For your final pass, use each side of the sponge only once before rinsing it out. You can use a soft, dry cloth to polish off the haze that forms after about 40 minutes (see the right photo above). Misting the grout with water several times a day for two or three days will increase its strength and prevent cracking. But wait 10 days before applying any grout sealer—an important step that increases water and stain resistance.

Dennis Hourany owns Elite Tile in Walnut Creek, California.

Tiling over a Laminate Counter

■ BY DAVID HART

I tear out tons of tub surrounds and sheet vinyl every year and install ceramic tile. That type of remodeling makes up the bulk of my work. Other than an occasional mud-set floor, I use cementitious backer board as tile underlayment on walls and floors. After having mixed results with plywood, I found that backer board also works great for counter-top renovations.

The major advantage to installing backer board over an existing laminate countertop is that it keeps down the total cost of the tile installation. Instead of building a new countertop, I set the tile on a sheet of ¼-in. backer board that's screwed to the old laminate. The backer board provides a sturdy, stable substrate for the tile; it saves me a day (or more) of labor; and it can knock several hundred dollars off the total cost of the project. (Obviously, this method won't work on postformed counters.)

Why not install the tile directly on the countertop? It doesn't work. I learned the hard way that latex- and polymer-modified thinsets don't bond well to plastic laminate, even though a mortar manufacturer assured me that they would. After two installation failures involving only thinset, I now over-lay the laminate with backer board and haven't had a callback since.

Make Sure the Original Counter Is Sound

Because a new sink is often part of a counter renovation, my first step is to determine the size of the new sink cutout. If the new sink is smaller than the original, I have to rebuild the counter to give the sink proper support before overlaying the top with backer board. If the new sink dimensions are larger, I cut the countertop to the correct size and con-tinue with the installation. (It's also worth noting here that unless they have flexible water supplies, most sinks need to be replumbed due to the increased depth of the counter.)

I also check the condition of the counter's particleboard. Prolonged exposure to steam from a dishwasher or water seepage from around the sink can turn particleboard into little more than loose sawdust. The best way to check is to crawl into the base cabinet and examine the underside of the countertop with a flashlight. If I can dig particleboard apart with a screwdriver or pocketknife or if it's swelling from exposure to moisture, then the damage is probably too severe to use this installation method. Scrap the existing top, rebuild it and quit reading this chapter.

All laminate countertops will move when you pound a fist on them, but excessive movement will lead to cracked grout joints and, eventually, loose tiles. Cement backer boards help tighten any floor or countertop if installed properly, but bouncy or spongy tops need to be fixed or scrapped. Often, a few screws driven up into the countertop through the cabinets' corner brackets will stiffen a bouncy top.

It's also important at this early stage to measure the height of the tiles that cover the edge of the counter (called V-cap) and compare that dimension to the height of the countertop's finished edge. The V-cap should cover the countertop edge and backer board. A typical V-cap covers about 1¾ in., which doesn't leave much tile hang-ing below the substrate; some run deeper, and others run a little shallower. I also make sure the cabinet drawers don't hit the tile overhang.

Cutting Cement Backer Board

If I need to keep the job site clean, some-times I cut backer board with a utility knife and a straightedge. Although it's slightly more expensive than other backer board, Durock (see "Sources" on p. 75) is somewhat softer and easier to cut with a standard utility knife. Yes, I burn through blades, but it's quick and virtually dust-free.

Utility knives don't work well on harder, slicker boards such as WonderBoard (see "Sources"), so to cut those types of board, I

Cut and Fit the Backerboard

Cutting backer board with a grinder is dusty but quick. Although backer board can be scored with a utility knife and snapped, an angle grinder fitted with a diamond blade cuts a cleaner line faster.

Narrower edge strips are more easily concealed. To ensure that the tile covers the backer board, the author keeps the edge strips at least ¼ in. back from the counter's edge.

rely on a right-angle grinder with a 4-in. dry-cut diamond blade (see the left photo on the facing page). A vital piece of equipment for compound or circular cuts as well, this tool throws a cloud of dust anytime I cut cement board with it, so I never use it in an enclosed space.

I always lay the board in place dry to check the fit; I usually allow up to a ½-in. gap between the counter and wall and up to a ¼-in. gap between individual pieces of board. The important thing here is that I don't want the backer board to extend beyond the edges of the top. After I cut the backer board to fit the existing top, I cut strips for the counter's edge about ¼ in. narrower than the edge of the countertop (see the right photo on the facing page) so that the backer board doesn't stick out below the bottom of the edge cap.

Modified Thinset and Screws Make a Better Bond

By itself, ¼-in. backer board offers no additional strength when attached directly to the substrate; a layer of the thinset beneath the backer board fills the voids and creates a vacuum that is nearly impossible to break. I never skip this step. Unmodified mortar doesn't provide any bond to the laminate, although it will stick to the backer board, so I always spend the few extra dollars and get latex or polymer-modified thinset, which cures harder than unmodified mortar and allows a small amount of deflection.

It's important to mix thinset with the proper amount of water. As a rule, too much water will create a weak bond; too little makes the product tough to trowel, and it

Glue and Screw to the Countertop

An autofeed screw gun speeds a tedious job. Faced with a day of driving screws into substrate, the author uses an autofeed screw gun that starts and seats each screw much faster than by hand.

Thinset increases the bond. Like peanut butter spread between two pieces of bread, thinset troweled onto the counter will fill voids beneath the backer board and strengthen the substrate.

may not bond to the tile or backer board properly. I try to mix it so that it has a smooth, creamy consistency. If the mix clings to my trowel without running off and still spreads easily, then I know I've got a good mix.

After mixing a batch of thinset, I trowel it onto the counter (see the left photo on p. 73) with a ¼-in. notch trowel, trying not to spread more thinset than I can use in 10 minutes or 15 minutes. For an experienced tilesetter, that can mean the entire counter, but for those new to this type of work, that might mean covering a small section at one time. Once a section of counter is covered, I lay the backer board in place and screw it down.

Because the board is only ¼ in. thick, I use screws that are 1 in. long. Longer screws might protrude through the bottom of the particleboard and give someone a nasty scrape. I like to space the screws about 6 in. apart on the perimeter of the board and 8 in. to 10 in. apart on the inside. Although I have used loose screws and a screw gun, I usually rely on a Makita® (see "Sources") autofeed screw gun (see the right photo on p. 73); it's just quicker. I try to make sure that there are no bubbles in the backer board and that I seat the screw heads flush or slightly below the surface.

Tile Layout: Big Tiles Are Better

Once the counter is ready, I take time for a careful tile layout. Nothing will ruin an installation more than a poor layout. For this project, I first installed the 6-in. V-caps, starting from the outside corners and working toward the wall (see the left photo below). I butter the backside of each tile as I go, which makes the next step cleaner.

Once the edge is complete, I lay out the interior tile pattern dry (see the right photo below) to see which tiles will have to be cut.

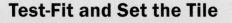

Test-Fit and Set the Tile

Layout starts from the center. To ensure a well-spaced layout, the author places whole tiles across the space, using a center mark as a reference. The remaining space is divided into two partial tiles.

V-caps go on first. These narrow, right-angle tiles form a border for the square field tiles. Starting at the exterior bullnose corners, the V-caps are laid out in an equal pattern that ends at a wall or a mitered inside corner.

Finish Up with Grout

Grout works best when spread in small areas. Worked into tile joints with a rubber float, grout tends to set up quickly, and it becomes difficult to remove from the tile surface. A clean, damp sponge is the best tool to wipe excess grout from tiles and to smooth grout lines.

On a perfect installation, I would end up with full tiles across the full width of the counter, but that never happens. The best installation will have the largest tiles possible in the most visible areas. And I'll often try to cut a small amount from tiles on both sides of the layout rather than cutting a large amount from the tiles on one side.

Once I've checked the layout, I start applying enough thinset to keep me going for about 10 minutes. If the mix sits on the backer board for much longer than that, it starts to skim over, and then it won't bond with the tile.

Apply Small Areas of Grout

After the tile is set, I wait a day for the thinset to cure before I start grouting. Most grout has a modifier in it, which creates a stronger, more stain-resistant grout, so there's no need to add latex to the dry powder. The grout–water mix should be stiffer than toothpaste but loose enough to push across the tile without great force.

Using a rubber float, I usually won't spread more grout than I can work in about 10 minutes (see the left photo above). I don't allow the grout to sit on the tile surface for long, either; once it has hardened, the grout is difficult to remove. I use a large damp sponge to smooth the joints and to wipe off the face of the tile (see the right photo above). It's important not to wipe too much out of the joints, to rinse the sponge frequently and to wring the excess water out of the sponge. Too much water can discolor or weaken grout.

David Hart is a tile contractor and outdoors writer living in Centreville, Virginia.

Sources

U.S. Gypsum
800-874-4968
www.usg.com
Durock

Custom Building Products
800-272-8786
www.custombuildingprojects.com
WonderBoard

Makita
800-462-5482
Autofeed screw gun
www.makita.com

Tiling a Backsplash

■ BY TOM MEEHAN

Saturday is estimate day at our store, Cape Cod Tileworks. Of the five or six estimates we do on Saturday mornings, at least a third of them are for kitchen backsplashes. Whether the room is new or old, a backsplash is a great opportunity to express a kitchen's qualities, including color, creativity, boldness, subtlety and craftsmanship. If you haven't done a lot of tiling, a backsplash is a great way to get your feet wet.

Layout: A Road Map for the Backsplash

Once the tile has been selected, the next step is layout. For this project, my client chose tumbled-marble tile. Its coarse natural texture makes a particularly nice contrast to a smooth, shiny kitchen countertop, such as granite.

The layout for most of this backsplash is fairly simple: three courses of 4-in. by 4-in. tile topped off by a narrow border; a filler course takes care of the space between the border and the wall cabinets. The challenging part is the patterned area behind the stove. Taller and more intricate than the rest of the backsplash, this area requires a layout that is dead-on accurate. My first step is measuring the exact dimensions of that space.

Over the years, I've found that doing the layout directly on the wall doesn't work well. Instead, I draw a full-size layout of the patterned area on a sheet of cardboard. Then

Tile transformation. A tile backsplash can lift an ordinary kitchen to extraordinary heights. Here, tumbled marble is the perfect complement to granite countertops and cherry cabinets.

I cut and arrange all the tiles as needed to fit the layout. I don't start to set tile on the wall until the test-fit is complete. This backsplash features small square dots at the intersections of the diamonds. At this point, I mark and cut these types of elements as well.

If a backsplash is interrupted by a window, it looks best if the tiles on each side of the window are the same size, which often means using partial tiles elsewhere. I plan the size and location of these partial tiles to please the eye.

Electrical outlets have to be incorporated into most backsplashes. A symmetrical lay-out around an electrical box looks best and is the easiest to cut. In extreme cases, the box can be moved for a proper-looking layout.

Install the Tile in the Right Order

Before mud and mastic start flying, it's critical to protect appliances, countertops and other finished surfaces. For this installation, a rubber shower-pan liner and a piece of cardboard protect the countertop and floors. The rubber liner is great because it can take a little impact if something is dropped on it. It also stays put, unlike a plastic drop cloth.

Test-fit the tiles on a flat surface. For the area above the stove, the author first measures the exact dimensions. Then he transfers them to a sheet of cardboard, where all the tile is dry-fit. Decorative elements such as the border and the square accent tiles are cut and fit at this time.

When I'm ready to set tile, I spread all-purpose mastic on the wall using a trowel with ¼-in. by ¼-in. notches (see the photo above). Because the tumbled marble for this backsplash is a fairly light color, I used non-staining white mastic, which prevents the tile from spotting or darkening.

I set the bottom course of tiles for the backsplash first, after putting spacers under the tiles to keep them ⅛ in. above the counter. If the counter has to be replaced in the future, this space provides enough room to slip in the new countertop without disturbing the backsplash.

To install each tile, I press it tightly against the wall about ¼ in. from its final position, then slide it in place to ensure a tight bond.

With the bottom course in place, I turn to the trickiest part of the job, the patterned area behind the stove. Border pieces go in first. To create visual interest, I like the border to stand slightly proud of surrounding tiles, a subtle strategy that's not difficult to do. Before installing each border piece, I butter the back with mastic. When the tile is pressed in place, the extra mastic makes the border stand out slightly from the rest of the tile. Setting a few of the regular backsplash tiles outside the border helps keep the border pieces straight.

As I place tiles, I make the grout joints roughly ¼ in. wide. Because these tiles are irregular, the joint size varies somewhat. Instead of relying on spacers, I shift the tiles slightly as the different sizes require.

For the diamond pattern of the backsplash, I install the tiles in a diagonal sequence to keep them aligned along their longest straight edge. The tiny square accent pieces go in as I set the larger diamond tiles.

Once the stove backsplash is done, the rest of the job goes quickly. The main backsplash is only four courses high, and it's fairly easy to keep the grout lines level and straight.

As for the cut tiles that fit against the end walls and upper cabinets, I cut them for a tight fit with little or no grout joint. Grout is most likely to crack where different materials meet.

Seal the Tile before Grouting

I leave the tile overnight to let the mastic set up. The next day, I wipe down the backsplash with a good impregnator/sealer, which helps protect the marble and acts as a grout release. Grouting tumbled-marble tile

Start at the border. To make the border tiles stand slightly proud of the rest of the tile, the backs receive a coat of mastic first (below). This will cause the tiles to stand out from the rest of the field when they're pressed into place (bottom).

To install a tile, press it against the wall and slide it about ¼ in. into position. Align diamond-shaped tiles along their long edges.

Working around an Electrical Outlet

Symmetrical coverage looks best when tile meets an electrical box. Mark the edges of the box on surrounding tiles and cut them to fit.

Cut the tile so that the ears on the outlets and the switches overlap the edges of the tile. Before installing the tiles around the box, back out the screws that secure the outlets and switches. Longer screws may be necessary to make up for the added thickness of the tile.

is a little more difficult than grouting standard glazed tile. Grout tends to catch and collect along the irregular edges and on the surface of tumbled marble as well as in the relief of the border tiles.

I always use sanded grout with tumbled marble. Sand mixes with portland cement to add body and strength to the grout, making it superior at filling the wide joints between irregular tile edges. Border tiles like the ones in this project also demand a stronger grout because they sit farther out than the rest of the tile.

I mix a stiff but workable batch of grout that won't fall out of the joints as I float it on in a generous coat. When all the joints are filled, I let the grout sit until it is firm to the touch, usually 15 minutes or so. Then I wipe the tile with a grout sponge dampened with clean water. I make sure to wring out the sponge before wiping the tile; too much water can dissolve the cement and weaken the grout. When cleaning marble tiles, I pay extra attention to rough spots in the marble and to the patterned areas in the border tiles. These areas may need a little more effort to remove excess grout.

After washing it, I let the grout set up for another 15 minutes (less, if the room is warmer than normal). Then I use a clean terry-cloth towel to wipe the grout haze off the tile surface. At this point, I also use a putty knife to remove any grout stuck in corners or in other places where I want to see a clean, straight grout line.

The next day, I do a final cleaning with a good tile cleaner. Because some cleaners corrode or stain, I keep the countertop, stove and sink protected. A day or two after cleaning, I finish the job by applying sealer to the tile and grout. If the tile is stone (as in this case) and I sealed the tile before grouting, an additional coat of sealer also protects the grout. I apply the sealer with a disposable foam brush and give the backsplash behind the stove a couple of extra coats to protect the tile and grout from grease.

Tom Meehan is a second-generation tile installer, owner of Cape Cod Tileworks in Harwich, Massachusetts, and co-author of Build Like a Pro® Working with Tile *(The Taunton Press, Inc., 2005).*

Cutting Ceramic Tile

■ BY DAVID HART

If it weren't for the cutting, tile work would be relatively easy. But tile is both hard and brittle—about as unforgiving as a material can be—and you always need to cut tile during an installation. Luckily, specialized cutting tools and techniques make this job much easier and can keep a potentially beautiful tile job from becoming a mediocre one.

Because the tools are specialized, though, more than one type of cutter is needed to complete all but the most basic installations. I never show up on a job with fewer than three different tile cutters. Also, remember that working with tile is like breaking glass all day long: Safety glasses are a must, and gloves are a good idea.

Cutting Boards: A Basic Straight-Cut Tool

Manual cutting boards are easy to use and cut most common types of ceramic tile. These simple cutters work much like a glass-cutter and use a carbide wheel mounted on a handle to score the tile's ceramic surface. After the tile is scored, the same handle is used to snap the tile along the scored line (see "Using a Cutting Board" on the facing page). I can cut a tile this way in seconds, and I have to set only the cutting board's stop to make repeated cuts.

Cutting boards are available in a variety of models that handle up to 20-in.-wide tiles. I own a smaller board, which cuts tiles up to 10 in., and a larger two-rail model, which has a 20-in. capacity. Both cut tiles on a diagonal, although a wet saw makes those cuts faster and cleaner.

The boards don't require more maintenance than an occasional drop or two of oil along the rail; the cutting wheels are replaceable and usually cost less than $15*. The cost of a cutting board can range from $30 for the smallest size to more than $300 for an imported cutter that handles 24-in.-sq. tiles.

Cutting boards have limitations: They cut only straight lines. Sometimes the break can veer from the scored line, resulting in a tile that has to be recut or finished with another tool. Cutting boards also can't cut marble, stone or thick quarry tile, and they can't take off a thin sliver of tile.

Using a Cutting Board

Under light, even pressure, the cutting wheel scores a line across the tile's surface (left). The handle is then levered down onto the tile, snapping it along the score (right).

One Tool Won't Do the Job

The tools shown here all cut tile but work best when used together. The cutting boards are portable; the wet saws make the cleanest cuts; and the nippers fit in your pocket and are used to remove waste or to fine-tune a cut.

Wet saw

Nippers

Large-capacity cutting board

Cutting board

Nippers Take Care of the Details

Another essential tile tool is a pair of nippers (see "One Tool Won't Do the Job" at left), sometimes called biters. Nippers are used to break pieces from tile, and as the name suggests, they work best when they take small bites. A common mistake when using nippers is to take too big a bite, which usually cracks the tile in half. Also, instead of crunching through the tile, I've found that nippers work better if you grab the tile and lever down, snapping off the piece.

If a pipe falls on a joint between two tiles, I use nippers to cut an arc in the tile. I also use them to trim off a thin slice from tile that my cutting board can't break (see "Cutting Tile with Nippers," below). You can pay $10 or so for a cheap pair of nippers, but for an additional $15 or $20, you get a better-quality model that features carbide-tipped jaws. Remember to be careful when you use nippers: The tile's cut edges are as sharp as broken glass and can easily slice an unwary hand.

Cutting Tile with Nippers

Cutting boards can score but can't snap a thin offcut, a job perfectly suited to nippers. Grabbing the waste and levering down with the nippers (left) usually produces a clean break. Any remainder can be nipped away as needed. When breaking out a small radius (right), it's better to take small, measured bites, especially as you get closer to the line. Large bites tend to crack the tile.

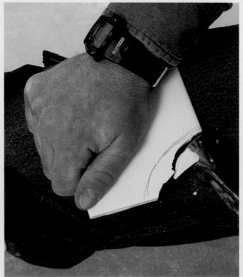

Making a U-Shaped Cut

Tile often must be cut to fit around light switches or soap dishes. Although nippers or a dry saw might work, a wet saw makes the cleanest cut. With the tile held flat on the saw bed, the two parallel cuts are made (see the photos at right) by pushing the tile into the blade.

To make the crosscut, many professionals might lift the tile into the blade. However, saw manufacturers recommend that the sawblade be plunged into the tile instead. After loosening the saw head's depth adjustment, you raise the head and turn over the tile. Aligned beneath the blade, the tile is held firmly while the blade is plunged into the cut (see the photo below).

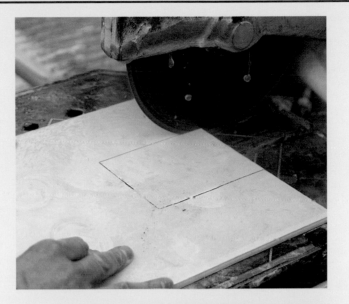

Sources

Below is a partial list of tile-saw, blade and tool manufacturers. A number of tool-supply houses on the web carry a wide selection of tile tools.

Makita
800-462-5482
www.makita.com

Target Tile Saws
800-288-5040
www.targetblue.com

Q.E.P.™ Co. Inc.
866-435-8665
www.qep.com

Superior™ Tile Cutter
310-324-3771

Crain Tools
408-946-6100
www.craintools.com

Felker® Saws
800-365-4003
www.felkersaws.com

MK® Diamond Saws
800-593-6095
www.mk-diamond.com

Rubi Tools USA Inc.
866-USA-RUBI
www.rubi.com

Cutting a Radius

To cut around a closet flange, the author makes straight cuts by holding one end of the tile on the bed and carefully lifting the other end into the blade (right). (Although not sharp, diamond blades should be treated with caution.) The waste is removed at the line with nippers (below).

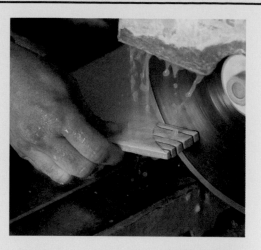

Wet Saws Are Messy but Make the Cleanest Cut

Wet saws are simple to use and versatile. I can cut fairly precise semicircles and other complex shapes with the help of a pair of nippers (see "Making a U-Shaped Cut" on p. 85 and "Cutting a Radius," above. Some cuts aren't easy, and I've gone through three or four pieces of tile before I successfully completed the cut. (That's why it's important to buy extra tile.) I can do some jobs, especially those with small tiles, without a wet saw; but for installations of large, thick or hard tiles, I have a wet saw ready to go.

The saws typically consist of a 1-hp (or larger) motor mounted over a shallow tub filled with water. The motor powers a diamond blade, usually 8 in. or 10 in. in diameter; a small pump sprays water onto the blade to cool and lubricate it and to keep tile dust

Forget a white pencil? When you're marking dark tiles, a pencil line drawn on a piece of tape becomes a good substitute for a grease pencil or a crayon. The mark can be full length on the tile or just serve as a crow's foot.

to a minimum. The tile sits on a sliding table that rides just above the water on a pair of rails.

To make a cut, I keep the tile flat on the sliding table and push the tile into the spinning blade under even pressure. The best way to make precise cuts is to mark the cut on the face of the tile with a regular pencil or a grease pencil. On dark tiles, I stick masking tape to the tile and mark the tape.

More than a dozen manufacturers make various styles of wet saws (see "Sources" on the facing page). They all cut tile, but I discovered that the smaller tabletop saws that retail for a few hundred dollars just don't perform as well as larger, more expensive models, which can sell for $1,000 or more.

I bought a tabletop wet saw when I first started my business and got rid of it two weeks later. It worked well enough, but it lacked a substantial blade guard and threw tile chips and water all over me. If you plan to take on several tile jobs over the course of a few years, it might be worthwhile to buy a larger wet saw. My Target® wet saw (see "Sources") has served me well for 15 years.

Don't want to drop $1,000 on a tile saw? If you plan to do only one or two jobs, you can rent a wet saw for as little as $40 or $50 a day at most tile distributors or home centers. With a little planning, you can do the necessary cutting in a day or two, no matter how large or complicated the job.

Dry-Saw Cutting

An angle grinder fitted with a diamond blade makes quick work of freehand tile cuts, but this tool is noisy, throws lots of dust and should be used outside with a dust mask. To cut a radius, the author firmly secures the tile with one hand, and holding the grinder in a tight grip throughout the process, he makes a series of shallow, scoring cuts along the pencil line. The shallow cuts keep the blade from binding in the material; as the blade progresses down into the material, the kerf should be widened toward the waste to allow the blade easier passage.

Cutting Holes with a Dry Saw

Bathtub plumbing often exits the wall in the middle of a tile. If a hole saw isn't handy, the next best thing is a dry saw. The angle grinder offers a quick, if rough, way of cutting a hole in the middle of a tile.

After measuring a square that's large enough to fit around the pipe but small enough to be covered by the flange, the author marks the tile on both sides and makes four small plunge cuts into the back of the tile (see the large photo below). The front of the tile must be checked periodically to make sure the cuts don't go beyond the lines (see the small photo below).

When the cuts on the back have extended nearly to the corners drawn on the front, the tile is flipped, and the cuts can be finished from the front.

Other small wet saws use an angle grinder equipped with a 4-in. or 5-in. blade, a tub of water and a small rolling tray. Like the first wet saw I bought, these saws work. But they have limitations, and I don't know a single full-time tile contractor who uses one.

No matter what type of wet saw I use, I always set up outside or in an area that can get wet and dirty. I never set up the saw over hardwood flooring (leaks from the saw's water tray stain wood), and I don't use it in a finished house for fear of damaging walls or flooring with the dust and water that inevitably spray from the blade.

Dry-Cutting with Angle Grinders and Diamond Blades

One of the best innovations in the tile industry is a dry-cut diamond blade that fits on an angle grinder (see "Dry-Saw Cutting" on p. 87 and "Cutting Holes with a Dry Saw" at left). Granite, marble, limestone, ceramic and quarry tile cut as if they were butter with this setup. I use a 4-in. blade on a Makita grinder (see "Sources") that has a fast blade rotation and can make fairly straight cuts, curves, L- and U-shapes and holes in the middle of a tile.

My angle grinder has limitations. It tends to chip the glaze on most ceramic tile and it leaves a rough edge on a piece of marble or granite. I don't use it when that cut edge is to be exposed.

Dry-cut saws are also fairly dangerous if they aren't used properly. Because the grinder has a tendency to jump when it starts to cut, it's important to hold tightly onto this tool. Grinders are equipped with a blade guard that some tile installers remove. I've always kept on the blade guard, and on a couple of occasions when the tool kicked back and hit me in the leg, the blade guard probably saved me from a trip to the hospital.

These tools also throw clouds of dust, so I use them outside unless the situation

Cutting the Perfect Hole

A diamond-coated hole saw chucked into a ⅜-in. drill cuts a clean hole in most ceramic tiles. Available in different diameters, hole saws are a bit slower cutting than dry saws. They also can't cut harder tiles or granite as easily but are still a good choice for production work.

requires indoor use. For instance, I've used my grinder to cut installed tile to retrofit electrical outlets, floor vents and even plumbing fixtures. When I cut indoors, I have an assistant hold a vacuum cleaner behind the blade to suck up the huge amount of dust that accompanies these tools. A vacuum won't get it all, however, so I cover anything that needs to stay dust-free.

Angle grinders are standard tools among professional tile installers, and anyone who plans to do several installations should consider purchasing one. The grinder itself costs $100 or so; the blade costs about $50.

Hole Saws for a Perfect Circle

If I want to cut a hole in the middle of a tile for a plumbing-supply line, I sometimes use a hole saw (see "Cutting the Perfect Hole" above). These tools have a carbide or diamond-tipped pilot bit and a diamond-edged hole saw, and they can cut through a soft-bodied ceramic or marble tile in less than a minute.

However, they don't work well on extremely hard ceramic tiles, marble or granite unless you use a hammer drill, and even that doesn't always cut through the hardest tiles. Costs range from $30 to $80. Hole saws come in several sizes; I own a 1¼-in.-dia. model and use a dry-cut grinder for larger holes.

Price estimates noted are from 2002.

David Hart is a tile contractor and outdoors writer living in Centreville, Virginia.

Grouting Tile

■ BY DAVID HART

If there's one thing that most tile installers dislike, it's grouting. A monotonous, shoulder-wrenching task, grouting is often delegated to the low man on the totem pole. That's a big mistake. Nothing can ruin a top-notch tile installation quicker than a bad grout job. An inexperienced helper can leave shaded or splotchy grout, uneven joints or grout that can be scratched out of a joint with the stroke of a fingernail.

Years ago, white-wall grout was nothing more than portland cement mixed with water; floor grout was mixed on the job by combining fine white sand with cement in a 1:1 ratio. Latex or polymer additives weren't an option, so installers simply added water to the mix. It worked—tile that was installed 50 or more years ago remains intact in many homes—but it had its limitations. Color choices were usually limited to white, black or gray. These days, grout is available in a rainbow of colors.

Modern grout products are also stronger and easier to use. The only factors that need concern tile installers are the type of grout to use, the proper consistency of the mix, even application and a thorough cleaning. And they shouldn't forget additives and sealants.

The Width of the Joint Determines the Type of Grout

There are two basic types of grout: sanded and unsanded. Which one you use is usually determined by the width of the joint between the tiles. Unsanded grout is the product of choice for any tile installation where the joints are less than ⅛ in. wide, even on floor tile. The finish is smooth, and it is relatively easy to clean.

Primarily used in joints wider than ⅛ in., sanded grout (also called floor grout or joint filler) provides the necessary strength for joints up to ⅜ in. and even wider. Although you might get away with unsanded grout in joints slightly wider than ⅛ in., it's a poor

Epoxy Grout Is Not for Everyone

About 10 years ago, the new buzzword in the tile industry was epoxy grout. It still is the most stain-resistant grout you can find, which makes it a great choice for use on kitchen counters and in restaurants and medical facilities.

It is, however, an unforgiving material to work. It's sold as a two-part additive that's mixed with regular grout or as a two-part ready mix that can also be used as a setting compound; either way, you have to mix the entire batch at one time to maintain proper proportions. There's no mixing by eye. It can be used only with ceramic tile and can't be removed from a porous surface.

Cleaning is often a frustrating experience that involves removing excess grout with nylon scrub pads and lots of water (epoxy isn't water soluble). Here, timing is really important. If you clean before the grout has set, the sticky epoxy pulls out of the joints and smears all over; wait a few minutes too long, and you'll be hard-pressed to remove it with a hammer and chisel.

Epoxy grout is also expensive. A two-part mix that's added to a 25-lb. bag of grout costs about $100* and covers about 100 sq. ft. of 8-in. by 8-in. tile. A smaller batch of two-part ready mix costs about $30 per quart.

If this material were just difficult and expensive, I still might use it, but most regular grouts now include latex additives far superior to their counterparts of 10 years ago. Coupled with a good sealer, these newer fortified grouts are stain resistant and hold up well under normal household abuse. Given the extra expense, time and elbow grease required by epoxy mixes, I can't think of a good reason to use epoxy unless a customer requests it. I certainly wouldn't recommend it to any neophyte tilesetters.

bet. More than likely, tiny hairline cracks will form as a result of shrinkage, which is controlled by sand in the mixture.

As you might guess, the texture of sanded grout is rougher and a bit harder to clean. Although sanded grout is associated primarily with floor tile, it should be used on any tile with wider joints, no matter where it's installed. However, be prepared for a long day if you plan to grout a wall with sanded grout. Unsanded grout readily clings to vertical surfaces, but sanded grout tends to roll down the wall and end up in little piles on the floor. It's possible to use sanded grout in thin joints, too, but pushing the thicker mixture into tight grout joints can be a frustrating task that typically leaves small pinholes in the grout finish.

Unlike products of 10 years ago, most grouts on the market now include a latex or polymer additive that strengthens the grout and helps it resist staining. Although you can buy grout without admixes, I don't bother; I'd rather have the extra protection that admixes offer.

To determine the amount of grout you will need to buy, consult the chart on the back of every bag of grout, or ask the sales clerk at the tile distributor. Measurements are typically based on the square-foot coverage per pound of grout, so you need to know how many square feet the job is, how wide the joints are and how big the tile is. One pound of grout might cover 5 sq. ft. of 6-in. by 6-in. tile with ¼-in. joints; a 25-lb. bag of grout typically covers about 100 sq. ft. of 8-in. by 8-in. tile with ¼-in. joints.

A 25-lb. bag of white-wall grout costs $10 or $12, and colored grouts can cost a few dollars more. I've used a half-dozen different brands, and all seemed to work well; none stood out as inferior or difficult to work.

Essential Grouting Tools

Floats: You can't grout without a float. They're available in two varieties: floor floats and wall floats. Wall floats have a soft rubber pad, while floor floats are much stiffer. Although some contractors use both, I use a wall float for all my grouting; I've found that a floor float is too inflexible to get into tight corners. A good-quality float can cost $20 or more and should last up to a year for a full-time installer. Eventually, the edges of the float wear down and won't clean off the face of the tile well.

Margin Trowel: This spatula-shaped tool is essential for mixing grout and for scraping it out of corners and along baseboards. It's also good for cleaning your other tools at the end of the day. A typical margin trowel will run about $15 and will last for several years.

Sponges: A good-quality grout sponge will cost $5 or more, but it's an essential tool for which there is no cheap substitute. I always use large grout

sponges because they pick up and hold more grout than smaller ones, and that saves time.

Gloves: Although some tile installers never wear rubber gloves when grouting, I won't grout without them. I don't like to have wrinkled skin at the end of a long day and, inevitably, the dry, rough skin that follows. Frankly, there's no reason not to wear long rubber gloves. Although I have used grocery-store gloves, they're too thin and rip far too easily. I use a pair of heavy gloves sold at tile distributors that have lasted almost a year. They cost about $8.

Kneepads: If you plan to spend more than an hour on your knees on a tile floor, you need kneepads. It's foolish to work without them. A cheap pair can cost as little as $5, but you get what you pay for. I have a pair of plastic-capped, foam-lined kneepads from Alta® (see "Sources" on p. 97) that cost about $35, and they still protect me after three years of hard use.

Careful mixing controls the ratio of water to powder. Mixing grout is often a process of estimating by eye; water should be added gradually to the powder to achieve the right mix. Clean water and a clean bucket are important ingredients.

Proper consistency ensures long-lasting grout. It's important that the final mix have a stiff, toothpaste-like texture that's easy to work into joints. Too much water weakens the grout and makes it runny; too little water makes it set up too fast.

Successful Grouting Depends on the Right Consistency

One of the most important aspects of grout is the mix. Nothing can make the process of spreading grout more difficult than adding too little water to the powder. A stiff grout mixture can be nearly impossible to push across the tile and into the joints. Conversely, nothing can ruin grout faster than adding too much water.

I generally mix grout by hand with a margin trowel (see "Essential Grouting Tools" on the facing page) in a clean 5-gal. bucket (see the left photo above). When I need a large amount, I save time by mixing with a paddle bit chucked into a variable-speed drill. A word of caution here: Whipping the grout into a froth can create air bubbles that will weaken the mix, so go slowly.

Generally, less water is better. As the water evaporates from a typical mix, it leaves microscopic voids. Excess water takes up more space; when the water evaporates, it creates larger voids and weak grout.

What's the right water-to-grout ratio? Most contractors (me included) eyeball the right balance between powder and water. Grout manufacturers usually recommend a ratio when mixing a whole bag ("mix 25 lb. of grout with 3½ qt. to 4 qt. of clean water," for instance). But there are times when you won't use that much, so you have to estimate. I always add less water than I think I need, and then add a little more if necessary.

Both sanded and unsanded grouts should have a stiff, toothpaste-like consistency when completely blended (see the right photo above). The mix should be allowed to sit for about 10 minutes and then be mixed again, an important step called slaking. Slaking allows the ingredients to react and the color pigments to blend, creating a stronger grout with uniform color.

The Trick Is to Work One Area at a Time

Working within arm's reach, the author packs grout into the tile joints with broad sweeps across the tile face. Working diagonally on subsequent passes pushes the excess grout to the next area.

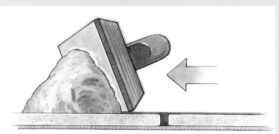

KEEP THE FLOAT AT AN ANGLE
To pack grout into joints, apply steady pressure with the float held at an approximately 45° angle. A second pass with the float held closer to 90° will clean excess grout from the tile.

Working the Grout into Place

Once I've mixed the grout a second time, I dump a pile of it onto the floor and start pushing it around with a float held up at about a 45-degree angle (see the drawing on the facing page). I want to make sure the joints are full, so I bear down on the float as I sweep it diagonally across the joints.

I grout a small area, as much as I can reach easily, then go back and pull the float hard diagonally across the tile, holding the float at almost a 90-degree angle. This step cleans off the large chunks of grout left behind and helps facilitate a quick cleanup later.

When I'm grouting walls, I usually load up a float with wall grout, start at the bottom and spread it up the wall (see the bottom photo at right), leaving plenty of grout on the face of the tile. I go back and clean off the excess grout by holding the float at a sharp angle and pulling it across the tile on a diagonal (see the top photo at right). As before, I push down on the float pretty hard as I pull it across the tile.

In average conditions, grout begins to set up in about 30 minutes, so I try not to spread more than I can work within that time. If I'm working in hot rooms or with porous tile, I spread just enough so that I can start the initial cleanup in 15 minutes to 30 minutes. I've also found that grout will set faster if left in the bucket, so I dump the entire mix onto the floor and keep it moving until it's gone.

Although cold joints aren't an issue with grout, there is a chance of color variation from one batch to the next. If I have to stop, I try to end at a doorway or clear delineation and feather the next day's work over the old.

Where Not to Grout

Grout won't crack between wall tiles that are properly installed, except at the junction of the tile and an abutting structure like a tub or a countertop. If I'm working with large

Wall grout starts at the bottom. To control the flow of grout, the author begins grouting low and works upward, packing the joints with a slightly angled float. As on the floor, a strong diagonal pass cleans up the excess.

tiles, I try to minimize the amount of grout I pack into these expansion joints. Otherwise, I grout everything, use a margin trowel or utility knife to cut out the grout before it hardens and then run a bead of latex-silicone caulk into the joint. Latex-silicone is easy to use and easy to clean up. Although it doesn't last as long as a pure silicone caulk, it does a fine job of protecting against water damage.

If you're concerned about matching that mauve or orange grout, most manufacturers now sell caulks that are color-matched to their grouts.

Cleanup starts with lots of sponge and little water. Once grout has firmed up in the joints, it's important to clean the tile and smooth the joints before the grout hardens. A damp sponge will clean up the majority of the grout.

A clean sponge picks up more grout. When the sponge's pores begin to clog with grout, the sponge should be rinsed and squeezed nearly dry. Excess water left standing on the joints will affect the curing process and discolor the grout.

Final Cleanup Needs Less Water

Cleaning up is as important as choosing and mixing the grout. The initial cleanup should accomplish two things: First, it should remove the bulk of the residual grout on the face of the tile; and second, it should smooth the joints without pulling out the grout.

When the grout in the joints has firmed up to where it isn't soft to the touch, I start cleaning. How long should firming up take? It varies with room temperature, humidity and the amount of water used in the mixture, but generally, it takes 15 minutes to 30 minutes. If I wait too long, the grout will dry on the face of the tile, and I'll have to scrape it off. In hot weather or direct sunlight, grout can stick to tile within 15 minutes.

I start with two buckets of clean water, a couple of large sponges, a margin trowel and a grout float. After wetting a sponge and wringing it out, I wipe the face of the tile and the joints with a light circular motion (see the photos at left), rinsing the sponge when the pores become clogged with grout. If the grout is pulling out of the joints, I wait a few more minutes. During this pass, I want to loosen the grout that's drying on the tile. To avoid splotchy color, I also make sure I don't leave puddles of water on the joints. I use a margin trowel to scrape clumps of grout out of the corners, door casings and any other place where it doesn't belong.

After I've smoothed the joints and loosened the grout stuck to the tile face, I go back with a bucket of clean water and remove the light grout haze that remains. With a clean, lightly dampened sponge, I wipe diagonally across the tile (see the photo on the facing page) for about 2 ft. or 3 ft., taking care not to push down too hard. I then turn over the sponge, repeat and rinse the sponge. This process takes time, and if I rush it, I end up smearing grout across the tile. Any streaks of grout haze left after the second wipe-down can be removed with a damp rag or mop when the grout has dried.

Second cleaning removes the grout haze. After the initial cleaning, the remaining grout residue can be wiped up with a clean, damp sponge and light strokes. It's important to rinse the sponge frequently during this stage.

Cleaning and Sealing Tile

Clients often tell me they want a maintenance-free floor, but there really is no such thing, at least not with tile, stone or marble. There is no substitute for general maintenance and upkeep; grout gets dirty, period. It's important to clean grout on a regular basis with a plastic-bristle brush and a commercial grout cleaner or a solution of mild soap and water. Make sure the soap isn't oil-based; products such as Pine-Sol® and Murphy® Oil Soap will darken the grout.

Sealers offer a way of protecting grout from stains; I usually recommend a sealer on floor installations. After trying several formulas available, I've found that the easiest to use is a water-based penetrating sealer such as TEC™ silicone sealer or TileLab® Grout & Tile Sealer (see "Sources" at right), which soaks into the grout and then dries without changing the appearance. (Sealer manufacturers recommend different waiting periods before sealer application, so consult the product literature first.)

No matter what type of sealer I use, it's often necessary to apply a fresh coat at least once a year, sometimes more often. After first cleaning the grout joints, I paint the sealer onto the joint with a foam or bristle brush, allow a few minutes for it to soak in and then wipe off any remaining liquid. I try not to let the sealer dry on the face of the tile, but if the sealer does dry, a quick scrub with a mild abrasive cleaner removes it. After I apply the first coat, I try applying a second coat; but often, it won't soak in. That's okay; it simply means the grout is properly sealed. If the second coat does soak in (the grout will turn dark as it would if it were wet), I simply continue with the rest of the wall or floor.

Other types of sealers include acrylic-based topcoats that leave a shiny film on the surface of the grout and oil-based sealers that will permanently darken the color of the grout. They all work, but each variety leaves a different finish on the grout. Just test the sealers in a hidden area first.

Water- and silicone-based sealers are the least expensive, running less than $20 for a quart. Oil and acrylic types can cost $40 a quart or more.

Price estimates noted are from 2001.

__David Hart__ is a tile contractor and outdoors writer living in Centreville, Virginia.

Sources

Alta
800-788-0302
www.altaindustries.com

TEC
800-TEC-9002
www.tecspecialty.com
TEC silicone sealer

Custom Building Products
323-582-0846
www.custombuilding-products.com
TileLab Grout & Tile Sealer

A Different Approach to Tiling Floors

■ BY TOM MEEHAN

"Hey, Dad, those dots down at the end are crooked," Christopher, my 5-year-old, observed while looking over my shoulder at a recent job. He was referring to the small square tiles that I was installing between larger octagonal tiles, and sure enough, those dots were crooked. I had to chuckle because Christopher's remarks sent me back 25 years, when I first tagged along with my dad on tiling jobs.

Back then, I figured I was a big help to my dad, but having one less kid underfoot was probably more of a help to my mom. Now I have my own tiling business, and I bring Christopher along on jobs when time and safety allow. As Christopher grows up, tools and techniques will continue to evolve. But proper prep work will always be the most important part of any tile job.

Take the Bounce out of Wood Floors

Most of the tile work I do these days is in houses with wood-frame floors, and there

are many approaches to laying tile on top of these floors.

To make a wood-frame floor structurally sound, I like to work with a substrate thickness of at least 1¼ in., which includes the subfloor and any underlayment. If I have doubts about the strength of a certain area, I check the floor for spring or movement by walking on it. Any give in the floor can mean cracked or loose tiles or loose grout in the future.

But floor stiffness isn't the only consideration when building up substrate to the proper thickness. Tile substrate also has to be stable. Some tile installers just put down layers of underlayment plywood to achieve the right thickness, and I've occasionally and reluctantly installed tile over this type of floor. My reluctance stems from the fact that wood expands and contracts with changes in temperature and moisture. On the other hand, tile moves very little and, when installed directly on top of plywood underlayment, can crack as plywood moves, especially at the seams between the sheets. Areas of high moisture, such as bathrooms and kitchens, are even more prone to under-layment movement.

If a bathroom or kitchen is small, I some-times use a layer of fibrous or cementitious backer board specifically made for ceramic tile. Backer board is more stable than ply-wood, installs quickly and bonds better to mortar. However, I don't think backer board is as rigid as plywood. So when I do use backer board, instead of using a single thick layer, I install a thin layer of backer board over a layer of plywood to make the sub-strate stronger.

But even when backer board or plywood is properly installed, the seams between sheets can telegraph to the tile as the sub-strate moves. Telegraphing, the most com-mon tile problem I see, can cause tile to crack or grout to loosen in conspicuous lines across the floor.

Concrete and Wire Mesh Make the Strongest Substrate

Probably the best foundation for tile over a wood-frame floor is an old-fashioned mortar bed, known in these parts as a mud job. In the simplest terms, a mud job involves lay-ing down a curing membrane of tarpaper on top of the subfloor with wire-mesh reinforcement and an inch or two of con-crete on top of that, depending on the spe-cific job. Aside from the messy installation, the biggest drawback to this method is the extra thickness it adds to the floor. In some cases the finished height of the floor could be 1½ in. to 2 in. above the subfloor, which can interfere with doors and create uncom-fortable, unsafe transitions between rooms.

If a client wants a tile floor to be the same height as an adjoining hardwood floor, a full mud job is usually out of the question unless proper adjustments in the subfloor height have been made early on. Recently, I tiled a foyer using a handmade, octagonal Mexican terra cotta, with small, square accent tiles. The height of the tile in the

Underlayment stiffens sub-floor. A layer of ¼-in. plywood glued and nailed to the sub-floor reduces the risk of cracked tiles.

foyer needed to be close to the height of the ¾-in. oak nosing that had already been installed at the top of the basement stairs.

The tile was ½ in. thick, which left me with limited space for underlayment. Because the foyer would see heavy traffic, I didn't feel comfortable using backer board. My solution was installing a modified mud job with a process that I've used successfully for over 20 years. This system creates a sub-strate almost as strong as a full mud job and

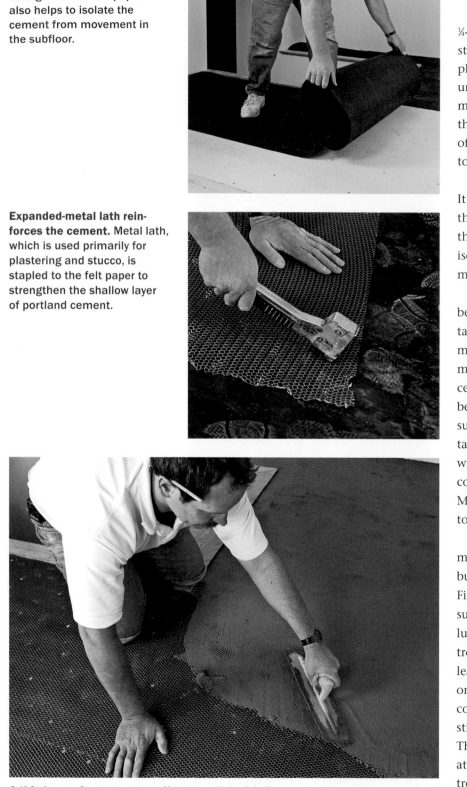

Felt-paper membrane isolates the plywood. A layer of felt paper keeps the plywood from drawing moisture out of the curing cement. The paper also helps to isolate the cement from movement in the subfloor.

Expanded-metal lath reinforces the cement. Metal lath, which is used primarily for plastering and stucco, is stapled to the felt paper to strengthen the shallow layer of portland cement.

A thin layer of cement tops off the mud job. A full mortar bed would be too thick for this floor. Instead, a thin layer of cement is troweled over some wire lath to complete the substrate.

keeps the finished floor at a reasonable height. More important, a modified mud job is stable and isolates the tile from any substrate movement.

I began by gluing and nailing in a layer of ¼-in. underlayment plywood to give extra strength and to act as a height filler (see the photo on p. 99). As with a full mud job, the underlayment was covered with a curing membrane of 15-lb. felt paper (tarpaper) (see the top photo at left). I overlapped the seams of tarpaper a couple of inches and stapled it to the underlayment every 6 in. to 8 in.

The tarpaper serves a couple of purposes. It lets the cement cure properly by keeping the plywood from drawing moisture out of the cement. Plus, tarpaper is the layer that isolates the cement and the tile from any movement of the plywood underneath.

In a full mud job, the next step would be laying down wire mesh on top of the tarpaper to reinforce the cement. But with my modified system, I stapled galvanized metal lath over the floor instead (see the center photo at left), overlapping the seams between the sheets about ¼ in. and making sure the lath was lying perfectly flat on the tarpaper. Metal lath is available at most drywall or masonry-supply stores and normally comes in 2-ft.-wide sheets, 6 ft. or 8 ft. long. Metal lath can be cut with ordinary tin snips to fit irregular shapes or spaces.

Next I covered the lath with a wet 50:50 mixture of portland cement and fine builders sand (see the bottom photo at left). Fine sand without pebbles is a must to make sure the cement goes over the lath without lumps. I spread the cement with a steel trowel in a smooth layer about ¼ in. thick, leaving no ridges and letting the trowel ride on the lath. When the cement was spread completely, the texture of the lath could still be seen through the cement in places. The next day, while the cement was still relatively fresh, I removed high spots with my trowel, and then I was ready to lay out and set the tile.

Dry-Fit the Tiles to Figure the Best Layout

The floor of the foyer would be seen from every direction—on entering the house, coming down from upstairs or coming up from the basement—so the tile layout was critical. The layout of the foyer tiles also determined the layout of the tiles on the basement-stair landing, which led to many more hundreds of square feet in adjoining basement rooms. To complicate matters, the handmade Mexican tiles were not uniform in shape and thickness and measured a nominal 8½ in. rather than the more convenient 8 in.

Instead of trying to lay out the tiles by measuring, I find it much easier and more effective to dry-fit the tiles on the floor (see the photo at right). By laying out a row of tile in each direction, I'm able to adjust the tiles to get the best layout. As a rule of thumb, the most important area in a tile layout is usually the area that's seen first and most frequently. In this case, I wanted a good-size piece of tile at the front door, but if I'd started with a full piece at the front door, there would have been an unsightly sliver of tile across the top of the stairway, which is the first place you look after you walk through the front door. So I laid out the first line of tile running front to back, splitting the difference to have good-size pieces of tile both at the front door and at the head of the stairs.

Using straightedges and a framing square, I laid out a second line of tile perpendicular to the first. I lucked out in the foyer because my perpendicular layout gave me a full tile at the bottom of the stairway to the second floor and a full tile against the wall next to those stairs.

When I was happy with my layout, I marked the floor at the edge of the tiles and snapped lines in both directions. Although I did my preliminary layout as carefully as possible, I had to tweak the layout lines a

Test-fit the tiles for the best layout. A good layout takes more than measuring. Dry-fitting tiles shows the tilesetter exactly how the tile will look in the most critical places.

little to get the snapped lines perfectly square to each other.

In this project my snapped lines revealed that the stairwell was about ½ in. out of square. But I was able to adjust the joints between the basement-stair nosing and the tiles, and once the tile was installed and grouted, the joints that I'd fudged were barely noticeable. When I was satisfied with my snapped lines, I snapped a couple of parallel lines a few courses over to keep the tiles running square and straight.

Another major consideration when laying out tile is waste. These Mexican tiles were not cheap, so I tried to lay out the tiles so that whatever waste I cut from a tile to fit it along one wall could be used along another wall somewhere on the job.

Use a Trowel with Bigger Teeth for Uneven Handmade Tiles

To make sure the tiles adhere well to the substrate, I try to obtain at least 85 percent mortar coverage on the setting surface, or the backside, of the tile (see the top photo below). Because the setting surfaces of these handmade tiles were not perfectly flat and because the tile thicknesses were varied, I chose a trowel with ½-in. notches to spread the mortar. The deep teeth on the trowel left high ridges of mortar that spanned the irregularities on the backs of the tiles and also ensured proper coverage (see the bottom photo below).

The foyer tiles were being installed over the modified concrete bed, so I used a standard thinset mortar that is mixed with water. I spread the thinset mortar up to my chalkline, taking care not to obliterate it. Then I pulled the trowel away from the line, maintaining full depth of the mortar at the edge of the tile where it lined up with the chalkline.

Beginning at the corner of my layout lines, I pressed the tiles into the freshly combed mortar along one of the lines (see the top photo on the facing page). I adjusted the tiles until the spaces between them appeared equal. Spacers that can be inserted between tiles are available at tile stores, but I don't like using them. The spacers are tough to get out once they're installed, and if left between tiles, they can interfere with grout.

When I was satisfied with the spacing, I filled in the field, starting at the perpendicular layout line and checking the pattern reg-

Proper mortar coverage. Some tiles are not perfectly flat, so the mortar ridges must be high enough to reach all parts of the tile's setting surface, as with the tile on the left.

Bigger teeth for higher ridges. A trowel with ½-in. teeth leaves mortar ridges high enough to reach all the parts of the tiles' uneven bonding surfaces.

Start the tiles at the layout line. Working back across the room keeps the tiles running straight and square from a snapped layout line.

ularly to keep my lines of tile straight and square. After installing two or three rows of tile, I went back and inserted the small square tiles between the larger tiles, making sure they'd pass the scrutiny of my keen-eyed 5-year-old.

The Mexican tiles were of three different clays, so the color varied significantly from box to box. To get a homogeneous blend of colors, I worked from several boxes at the same time.

A Wet Saw Offers the Easiest Way to Cut Some Tiles

The tiles along the outside wall and the stairs to the basement had to be cut to size. But because of their uneven surface, hand-made tiles cannot be cut well with a conventional score-and-snap tile cutter. Instead, I used a wet saw, arguably the most valuable tool in the tile-setting trade (see the photo at right).

A wet saw cuts through tile with a diamond blade. Tiny diamonds on the edge of a wet-saw blade make quick work of cutting through even the thickest tile.

A wet saw can make right-angle cuts or take small slices that are nearly impossible with a score-and-snap cutter. The edge of a wet-saw blade is encrusted with industrial diamonds that can cut through any tile. A fine water spray lubricates and cools the blade as it cuts. If you do a lot of tiling, a wet saw is a must. But even if you tile only occasionally, it's worthwhile to rent a wet saw for the job. At $50 a day, a wet saw can save you hours of aggravation and give your job a more professional look.

Tile nippers are another useful tile-cutting tool. They come in handy for fine cutting around obstacles such as pipes and corners. Nippers are basically pliers with opposed cutting jaws. They might seem easy to use at first, but it takes time and patience to get the hang of using nippers. The most important part of using nippers is removing just a little of the tile at a time. Grab the edge of the tile between the nipper's jaws and pull down while squeezing the handles together gently. I nibble away at the edge in this manner until I've removed all the waste.

Making room for the grout. Before the grout is spread, excess mortar that has oozed up between the tiles is taken out with a putty knife.

Fill in All Grout Joints

The day after I finished setting the tile, while the thinset was still relatively fresh, I went over the floor and took out excess thinset that oozed up in the joints between the tiles (see the photo below). A trowel or a stiff putty knife works well to remove these ridges. At the same time, I gave the tiles a good cleaning with water and a sponge to make the grouting easier.

Because I had so much tile to grout, I mixed 2 gal. to 3 gal. of grout at a time in a drywall bucket using a blade-mixer bit chucked into a ½-in. drill to speed up the process. Instead of water, I mixed the grout with a latex additive, and then let the mixture slake (rest or stand untouched) for five minutes before mixing it again. The additive strengthens the grout and makes it more water resistant once it sets up.

Epoxy grouts that are strong and stain-resistant are also available. However, these grouts are very labor intensive because of a more difficult cleanup process. I rarely use epoxy grout on floors, and because of the large scale of this project, I opted for the latex-modified grout instead. Epoxy grouts are not recommended for these handmade tiles.

Handmade tile is porous and can absorb moisture from the grout, making it set up more quickly. The latex additive is harder to absorb, so it keeps the grout from setting up too quickly. Damp weather can also lengthen setup time. If I have doubts, I grout a small sample section before attacking the whole floor. Also, I check to make sure the grout doesn't stain the tiles. The tiles I used on this project were sealed, so staining was not a problem. But other handmade tiles may have to be sealed before they are grouted; otherwise, you'll have a huge mess.

The basic trick to grouting is to fill all the joints before the grout starts to get stiff. I spread the grout in broad diagonal strokes with a rubber grout float working across the joints in the tile (see the left photo on the facing page). After going back and forth in

Spread the grout in broad diagonal strokes. To make sure all the joints are filled, the grout is pushed back and forth in large strokes across the tile joints.

A wet sponge cleans off the heavy residue. A wet sponge is used to remove the heaviest grout residue. Two or three washes are necessary before leaving the grout to set up.

A clean towel wipes away the haze. After the water dries and the grout has had a chance to set up, a terry-cloth towel removes the haze from the grout and brings out the shine.

opposite directions with the float, I pushed the grout into the highs and lows of the irregular terra cotta tile with the palm of my hand. Rubber gloves are a must for this step.

Next I gave the tiles a double wash with clean water (see the top right photo above). The first wash removed the heaviest grout residue, and the second neatened the grout joints. When the tiles were fairly clean, I let that area sit for about 15 minutes. It usually takes that long for the wash water to evaporate, leaving a film or haze on the tile. Then I wiped off the film with a clean terry-cloth rag (clean cheesecloth also works well) and brought the tiles to a shine (see the bottom right photo above).

Sometimes the haze doesn't come off the tiles with plain water, and a stronger cleaner may be required. I recommend trying full-strength vinegar first and using a sponge with a layer of mildly abrasive Scotch-Brite on one side to loosen stubborn grout residue. As a last resort, you can use a weak acid solution (about 1 part acid cleaner to eight parts water), but remember to rinse the tiles thoroughly with clean water after the acid wash or vinegar.

Like these handmade Mexican tiles, many tiles now come with an epoxy wear coating that keeps the tiles looking great for a long time. However, for tiles such as these, I suggest applying a liquid topcoat, also called a traffic coat, once or twice a year to renew and to help protect the finish. For cleaning these tiles, any pH-balanced cleaner works fine.

Tom Meehan is a second-generation tile installer, owner of Cape Cod Tileworks in Harwich, Massachusetts, and co-author of Build Like a Pro® Working with Tile *(The Taunton Press, Inc., 2005).*

Glass Tile

■ BY TOM MEEHAN

It has been used for centuries, but until recently, glass tile was relegated to museums and specialty shops. Today, it comes in an array of styles, from iridescent mosaics to luminous squares of recycled and sandblasted beer bottles (see "A Peek into the World of Glass Tile" on pp. 112–113). Tile shops like mine see glass-tile sales double every year. However, lots of folks are in for a shock if they try to install it like ceramic tile: The thinset and its application are different; the paper backing for small tiles is stuck to the front, not to the back of the tiles; and timing becomes an important part of the job.

Layout Needs Room to Move

On this particular job, the shower area was to be covered with 1-in. tiles grouped into 12-in.-sq. sheets. When I work with small tiles, I try to make sure that the backer board is smooth and flat; any imperfections will show as bumps in the tile. This phenomenon is especially true with glass tiles, which catch the light even more than ceramic or stone. Once I've installed the backer board, I seal the joints between the sheets with thinset and mesh tape, and then smooth any bumps with a steel floating trowel and thinset. The thinset should set overnight before the tile is installed.

When laying out a back wall, don't be tempted to squeeze the sheets together so that you can get a full tile and avoid cutting. Believe it or not, glass tiles expand and contract with changes in temperature, much more so than ceramic tiles. Direct sunlight can heat tiles enough to make them move. If tiles are too tight, any movement can make them pop off the wall or crack—or even crack the backer board. I try to leave ¼ in. of space in each corner; intersecting walls hide the gap.

I begin the layout with a level horizontal line halfway up the back wall, equivalent to an even course of tile, which in this case worked out to be 48 in. from the top of the tub. This horizontal line serves not only as a reference for spacing but also, as you'll see later, marks the extent of the first round of applying the glass tile. Next, I measure up to determine the width of the row at the ceiling. Anything over a half piece works well, and I can adjust the cut to make up the difference when the ceiling is uneven.

Thinset? Make Mine Extra-Sticky

Because it's vitreous, glass doesn't absorb liquid like ceramic tile, and it requires a higher grade of acrylic or latex-modified thinset to

Troweling

1. Spread thinset on the wall

Many glass tiles are translucent, so you need to use white thinset because gray will show through and darken the tile. With a ³⁄₁₆-in. V-notch trowel, roughly distribute the thinset over a small area (photo 1). Even out the material using the trowel's notched edge (photo 2), then smooth the ridges (photo 3) so that they won't show through the tile.

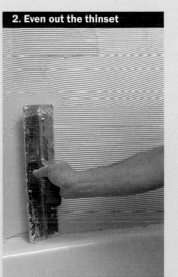
2. Even out the thinset

3. Smooth the ridges

bond to the backer board. Most glass-tile manufacturers specify what brands of thinset to use; on this job, I used Durabond Superflex (877-387-2266). Because the tile often is translucent, the thinset should be white; gray mixes darken the tile's color. Any pattern the trowel leaves in the thinset will show through, too, so the thinset must be spread and leveled with a ³⁄₁₆-in. V-notch trowel, and then smoothed out (see "Troweling" on p. 107).

I start laying the tile sheets from the level line, and then work down rather than working with a full sheet off the tub. If the tub is out of level, it's easier to adjust the cuts as measured from the course above. Once I press the sheets into the thinset and finish the half wall, I use a block of wood and a hammer to bed the tile fully and evenly into the thinset. You also can use a beater block (a wooden block padded on one side with a piece of rubber, available from most tile dis-

Setting

Many varieties of small glass field tile are held together in sheets by a paper facing on the front (photo 1) rather than a mesh fabric on the back. (Mesh on the back might be visible through the translucent material.) To make a wall of tile appear unified and not look like a grid of 12-in. squares, the paper must be removed and individual tiles adjusted to mask the pattern.

The trick lies in waiting for the thinset to become tacky; in normal conditions, this might be 15 minutes or 20 minutes. If the thinset is allowed to dry beyond that time, say an hour, the bond becomes more fragile, and more tiles will pull off with the paper. If the thinset is left to dry overnight, the bond sets, and the tile will be impossible to adjust.

The author first wets the paper with a sponge dampened with warm water (photo 2); after a few minutes, the water-based glue softens, and the paper can be peeled off gently (photo 3).

During the process of peeling the paper, individual tiles will fall off occasionally (photo 4). A quick coat of thinset on the tile's back is enough to set it back in place.

1. Set the tile

tributors) and a rubber mallet. I make any cuts with a wet saw (see the bottom right photo below) fitted with a diamond blade; a pair of tile nippers is handy to make minor adjustments in a cut.

Timing Is Crucial when Removing Paper Facing

The main reason I don't install too much glass tile at one time is that while the thinset is wet, I need to move individual tiles and erase any pattern inadvertently created by the 12-in. tile sheets. But first I have to

2. Dampen the paper

4. Make an easy fix

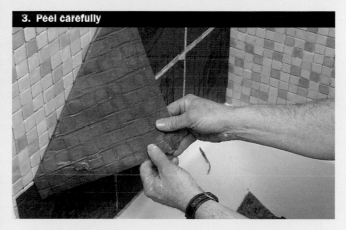

3. Peel carefully

Simple Jig for Cutting Small Tile

Cut with a wet saw, small glass tiles often are difficult to hold and cut accurately. The author makes an L-shaped cut in a larger piece of tile and uses it as a jig that holds the smaller tiles in line with the sawblade.

Grouting

Each tile manufacturer specifies what type of grout to use on a particular tile. After the grout is spread (photo 1) and has set up for about 20 minutes, the author wipes away the excess with cheesecloth or paper towels (photo 2). A sponge dampened with clean water (photo 3) works well to clean any residue from the tile.

1. Pack the seams

2. Wipe the excess

peel off the paper facing carefully so that I don't disturb the majority of tiles.

After waiting 15 minutes or 20 minutes for the thinset to bond, I wet the paper with a sponge and warm water. After a minute or so, the paper can be pulled off slowly, downward at an angle. One or two tiles may pop off, but that's no big deal; I just stick them back in place with a dab of thinset.

The trickiest part of this process is that the timing varies according to the room's temperature and humidity. Heat and dry

conditions make the thinset bond faster and give me less time to work, so I start to check the bond in an inconspicuous place after about 10 minutes. If the tiles move around too easily as I peel off a bit of paper, I know that I should wait a few more minutes.

Once the paper is off, the glass tiles must be examined to make sure none has slipped. Never wait until the next day to remove the paper; the tiles have to be examined and straightened while the thinset is fresh (see "Setting" on p. 108).

3. Clean the tile

Instead of using a specialized edge tile, the author sometimes runs the field tile to the wall edge and smooths any sharp edges with a diamond-impregnated pad.

When Grouting, Less Water Is Better

After the thinset has bonded fully for 48 hours, the tile must be washed to prepare it for grouting. I use a nylon-bristle brush and a sponge with warm water to clean any residue or paper backing from the surface of the tile. I use a utility knife to remove any excess thinset in the joints, but I'm careful when doing so; glass tile scratches easily.

Grouting glass tiles is not difficult, but again, it's different from grouting ceramic tile. Some manufacturers specify sanded or nonsanded grout; here, I used a recommended sanded grout in a color that complemented the tile. After I spread the grout on the walls, I let it set for about 20 minutes; the wait is longer than for ceramic tile because the glass tile doesn't absorb moisture from the grout.

Before starting to clean with water, I use cheesecloth or paper towels to rub down the walls to get rid of any extra grout and to fill in any voids between the tiles. This dry method also lets me clean the surface

A Peek into the World of Glass Tile

Glass tile is versatile stuff; it's available in styles that range from clear to opaque, from glossy and iridescent to the eroded look of beach glass.

Colors range from gaudy lollipop primaries to muted earth tones and just about every shade in between. Commonly seen in sheets of 1-in. squares, glass tile now is made in sizes that approximate ceramic tiles (2-in., 4-in. and even 12-in. squares), as well as rectangles, textured borders and tiny mosaics. And like ceramics, it can be used on walls, counters and floors, although glass tiles used on floors should have a matte finish or texture that makes them slip-proof.

One big factor to consider: Glass is more likely to show scratches than ceramics or stone; finishes applied to the tile are susceptible to scratches, too.

Prices range from $10* to $30/sq. ft. for some of the more common field tiles to upward of $100/sq. ft. for custom tiles.

Texture with a variety of color

These 4-in.-sq., clear-glass tiles have textured faces and ribbed backs; a glaze bonded to the tile backs gives them their color. The cost runs $60 to $80/sq. ft. The company also offers a higher-end integral color tile and custom designs.
Architectural Glass Inc.™
845-733-4720
www.architecturalglassinc.com

Earth tones in recycled glass

Made from 100% recycled content, Bedrock tiles are available in many sizes, from 2-in. squares to 5-in. x 10-in. rectangles to hexagonal shapes. Finish can be glossy or matte, but the color is integral and ranges from clear to solidly opaque. Price is about $90/sq. ft.
Bedrock Industries
877-283-7625
www.bedrockindustries.com

---

without adding any extra moisture that might dilute the grout.

Once the tile is wiped down, I go back over it with clean water and a damp sponge to do a finer cleaning and to reduce any topical film. Less water is better. As in any grouting job, it's important to strike corners or intersections of wall and tile with a trowel or putty knife to make sure these joints are tight and neat. Once everything is set and a slight film has developed over the tile, I use a rag to bring the glass tile to a shine. I try not to wait more than 15 minutes after sponging; any longer, and the film starts to set up and becomes too hard to remove easily (see "Grouting" on p. 110).

Cleaning and Sealing Are Just as Important as Thinset and Grout

A day or two after grouting, I smooth exposed tile edges with a diamond-abrasive pad, and then clean the tile with a commer-

Solid colors in mosaics

Hakatai sells mesh-backed mosaics (instead of paper-faced) in ¾-in. and 1-in. sizes in many opaque and solid colors, priced from $8 to $11/sq. ft. They also offer 2-in. squares of clear glass with color fired onto the tile back and irregularly shaped pebbles, both priced at $24/sq. ft. Hakatai Enterprises Inc.
541-552-0855
www.hakatai.com

Iridescence

Oceanside offers a variety of tile with an 85% recycled content, ranging from 1-in.-sq. mosaics to 5-in. x 5-in. field tiles, specialty borders and decorative single tiles. Many feature a metallic glaze that's applied to the surface of the tile. Prices for most mosaics and field tiles are in the range of $25 to $30/sq. ft.
Oceanside Glasstile™
760-929-4000
www.glasstile.com

Broad palette of recycled color

Sandhill makes mosaic, field and specialty tile from 100% recycled glass in 36 different shades of integral color, glossy or matte. They also offer custom border and mosaic designs. The price for stock tiles is about $60/sq. ft.
Sandhill Industries
208-345-6508
www.sandhillinc.com

cial tile cleaner. I wet down the walls before applying the cleaner and also protect any chrome or brass plumbing fixtures with tape and plastic bags. Rather than use stronger cleaners that might compromise the grout, I use a fine, nylon scrubbing pad to clean off heavy grout residue. I always give the walls a double rinse to flush away any cleaner residue.

Sealing grout is simple and should not be overlooked; it helps keep grout lines from absorbing mildew and other stains. I use a wet, clean cloth rag and apply a double coat of sealer on the grout and tile as well. I then towel off the wall with a dry rag. I used Miracle Sealants 511 Impregnator (800-350-1901) on this project. One key to sealing walls is to start from the bottom and work up from floor to ceiling to avoid streaking. Once the sealer is dry, glass-tile maintenance is minimal; I use dish soap and water to clean it on a regular basis.

*Price estimates noted are from 2004.

Tom Meehan is a second-generation tile installer, owner of Cape Cod Tileworks in Harwich, Massachusetts, and co-author of Build Like a Pro® Working with Tile (The Taunton Press, Inc., 2005).

Decorating Tile at Home

■ BY NANCY SELVIN

Bathroom bulletin board. Running kitties pass over a solitary dog on the tiles of this bathroom wall. The drawings were done by the author's daughter and then transformed into glazed-tile illustrations using photo-screen printing techniques.

Our little upstairs bathroom needed an overhaul. It was dark and mildewed, and it cried out for some bright, easy-to-clean surfaces. As a ceramic artist, I naturally wanted to work some tile into the bathroom. But I also saw the project as an opportunity to transform the bathroom into a page of our family album. I wanted the new tile to capture the exuberance of my 6-year-old daughter Liz's artwork.

Like lots of families, we had kid drawings on walls and stuck to the refrigerator door. On paper the drawings are fragile things that eventually get tucked away in folders. Captured on tiles, however, the images would be durable reminders of our long history in our home.

Liz and I went around the house picking out likely drawings for the bathroom. I also asked her to draw something especially for this project. She created the running kitty, which ended up as the top border of the tub-surround, and the purring kitty, which was just right for a series of tiles by the tub rim.

Picking the drawings was the easy part. Now we had to get them onto the tiles. I wanted to keep the process as simple as possible, so I had Liz's drawings reproduced photographically on screens, like those used to print logos and such on T-shirts (see the photos above). Using a special kind of low-temperature overglaze material called china paint, I used the screens to print her sketches on inexpensive store-bought tiles. When fired in a kiln, Liz's drawings were bonded to the tiles in deep, rich colors.

Screen Printing

Stretch a piece of tightly woven silk or polyester over a wood frame, and you've got a screen for printing. Adhere an emulsion of the image that you want to reproduce on the backside of the screen, and you're ready to print. The emulsion creates the negative of the image, and it blocks the passage of ink through the remaining area of the screen. During printing, the ink passes through the unblocked portions of the screen, duplicating the image onto the work surface. (There are many ways to make screens and to apply the emulsions. If you want to know more about the different methods, your art-supply store should have the information necessary to get you started.)

I took the easy way out and let our local screen-printing shop make the screens and take care of the photography and the emulsion work. This service can usually be provided by any well-equipped screen-printing shop. Prices for screens vary, depending on size. To give you a ballpark idea, an 18-in. by 20-in. screen, including the photography and the emulsion work, currently costs about $60* in our area.

For this project I specified #14 denier polyester for the screen because it has the optimum porosity for printing china paint. It's important to know if the shop uses a water- or a solvent-based emulsion. Using the wrong ink (or the wrong cleanup materials) can dissolve the image. A water-based emulsion will dissolve a water-based image, and a solvent-based emulsion will dissolve a solvent-based image. I was planning to use water-based inks and clean up with detergent and water, so I asked for solvent-based emulsions.

Blank Tiles and Overglazes

For our bathroom I chose glazed, 4-in.-sq. tiles, the color of newsprint, with a glossy finish. The off-white color fits my design concept, and glossy tiles make a good background for china paint. China paints fuse to the glazed tile at a lower temperature than that required to fire the tiles, so applying a china paint on top of an already finished, glazed tile doesn't change the tile's original finish.

Once we had the drawings picked out, I drew a grid that represented the tiles so that I could learn how many tiles the image would cover and where the grout lines would fall. Because the images were transferred photographically to the screens, I could have the drawings enlarged or reduced as needed to fit them on the tiles.

China paints come in dry pigment form and have to be mixed with a printing medium, such as glycerin, gum or squeegee oil, to make them into inks. I tried all three and learned that only the squeegee oil would adhere sufficiently to the tiles during firing. China paints and squeegee oils are available at most ceramic suppliers.

To keep the printing simple, I planned to reproduce each image in only one color. I chose a simple palette of bright red, mustard yellow, dark brown, teal blue and avocado green.

I mixed the oil and the powdered china paint in a porcelain mortar and pestle at a ratio of 2 parts (by volume) of color to 1 part #175 squeegee oil. The ratio of the mix isn't as critical as the consistency. It should be thick and gooey, like stiff molasses. I grind the colors ahead of time and store them in covered plastic containers.

Printing

I make a printing table by first affixing a pair of hinged jiffy-screen clamps to a ½-in. plywood base. The clamps hold the screen in place during printing and keep it from shifting while I lift the screen after each tile is printed. These clamps make it easy to switch screens.

I pencil registration marks onto the plywood to align each set of tiles. Some images, such as the running kitty, are printed on a single tile—bigger ones, such as the purring kitty, are printed on four tiles grouped tightly together.

I ready each tile for printing by wiping it with a rag and a little rubbing alcohol to ensure that no dust or fingerprints cling to the tile's surface. If the image doesn't come out just right, I clean the tile with an alcohol-soaked rag and start over.

Before I start printing, I run 2-in. plastic packing tape around the inside of the screen to seal the edge where wood meets fabric. This keeps ink from slipping under the frame during printing.

To print, I spread a thick ribbon of china paint on the screen just above the image and across its full width. The screen is lowered onto the tiles, which are aligned under the image. I select a squeegee that is wide enough to span the drawing. Holding the squeegee with both hands and using an even, downward pressure, I pull the color toward me, spreading the china paint and squeezing it through the screen (see the photo above). After the color passes over the image, I lift the screen off the tile and spread the china paint back across the screen, refilling the image with wet color so that it won't dry out while I position another batch of tiles.

After I've finished printing enough versions of one image, I unclamp the screen and quickly saturate it with dishwashing detergent (Blue Dawn® works best). With a sponge, I spread on soap directly from the bottle, then put the screen into the sink and rub it down with water to remove all traces

of the china paint. I've learned the urgency of this step the hard way. When a screen sits too long before cleaning, it's virtually impossible to clean, and the original clarity of the image is lost.

Firing

I let the printed tiles dry overnight in a dust-free atmosphere. China paint will lift up (referred to as crawling) in the firing if the oil hasn't sufficiently dried.

I place each tile on a spacer in the kiln and fire the loaded kiln slowly to 1,443°F (called cone .017 by ceramicists). During the initial stages of firing, I keep the kiln lid propped open and run the exhaust fan until the smell of the burning oil dissipates (leaving the lid on throughout the firing will muddy the colors). It takes approximately six hours to reach temperature. Then I let the kiln cool overnight. As soon as they are unloaded, the tiles are ready to install.

*Price estimates noted are from 1993.

Nancy Selvin *is a ceramic sculptor living and working in Berkeley, California.*

Tiling with Limestone

■ BY TOM MEEHAN

My wife, Lane, and I own a tile store on Cape Cod, so I've gotten used to seeing tile of many different colors, shapes and materials all in the same room. But I've never met a homeowner who wanted to turn a bathroom into a tile showroom. I did come close recently when I tiled a bathroom that combined striking black marble; gray granite; tumbled marble; and a large, colorful hand-painted ceramic mural. The unifying element that made this unlikely combination successful was limestone tile.

Sort the Tiles before You Mix the Mortar

As an experienced tile installer, I had the dream job of integrating all these different types of tile with limestone in a single room. Limestone, which can be fairly soft and porous, is usually a breeze to work with and has subtle, earthy tones that form a perfect complement to almost any type or color of material (see "Limestone's Origins: Fossils, Coral and Seashells" on p. 120).

Because the color of limestone can vary from tile to tile and from box to box, I begin by opening boxes and checking the tiles for differences in shade or slight veining that

might make one tile stand out from the rest. The differences are usually subtle, but a misplaced tile in a different shade can stick out.

As I went through the boxes of limestone tiles for this bathroom, I culled some tiles that had slightly different shades or that had chipped corners. I also came across some tiles with nice crystalline veins that I set aside to give large open areas, such as the floor or the shower walls, a monolithic look. Out of the 550 sq. ft. of limestone tile that I installed in this bathroom, only about 20 or 30 tiles were irregular in color or badly chipped. These tiles were set aside for cuts, and tiles with off colors were relegated to an inconspicuous closet floor.

To add interest to the layout, we decided to run the tiles diagonally on the horizontal areas (tub deck and main floor). The diagonal pattern contrasted the square layout of the wainscoting and the shower walls. For the floor, I figured that a 6-in. border (in black marble) would allow me to use more full tiles and fewer small pieces in the field.

To enhance the diagonal layout, I positioned 3-in. black-marble inserts at the intersection of every fourth tile. A pattern of inserts done this way is called a clipped-corner pattern because the corners of the

Limestone's Origins: Fossils, Coral and Seashells

Look at limestone under a microscope, and you'll see coral, seashells and the skeletons of sea creatures that accumulated over eons in the sediment on the ocean floor. Millions of years ago, the surface of the earth was changing dramatically. Mountains were thrust up out of the oceans, and the sediment on the ocean floor turned into limestone. Some of that limestone encountered tremendous geological heat and pressure, crystallizing and transforming it into marble.

Like marble, limestone occurs in a wide variety of textures and colors from grays, greens and reds to almost pure white. Far and away the most common color of limestone tile is a sandy beige like the tile used here. Even so, a single tile can have specific areas of contrasting color, and often you can see the full outline of a seashell or fossil in limestone's richly textured surface.

intersecting tiles are cut off to accommodate the insert. I centered the floor pattern in the area that would be seen first, in front of the raised-panel tub-enclosure face.

Another layout concern was the long exposed wall that holds the main door to the bathroom. To catch another full diagonal tile, I increased the border along that wall to about 6½ in. My objective was to give the appearance that the room was built to the size and dimension of the limestone tile.

The layout of the walls was relatively simple. Because the floor tiles ran diagonally, the walls and floor did not have to line up. I made it a point to avoid small cuts whenever possible and to put the fuller-cut tiles in obvious places such as inside corners. The mural was centered on the wall above the tub to give the feeling of looking out a big limestone and ceramic window at Cape Cod's scenic landscape.

A Wet Saw Is Indispensable

Working with limestone is similar to working with polished marble. However, marble is much less forgiving and is usually set in a perfect plane with no grout joint. But in most cases, limestone can look better with a fine grout joint. On this job, I left a ⅛-in. joint between the tiles.

Because limestone is part of a geological formation (sedimentary rock), it should be cut only with a wet saw equipped with a diamond-edge blade (see "Cutting and Installing Limestone" on the facing page). I precut as many pieces as possible, especially when the tile is being installed in a diagonal pattern.

As with most tiles, limestone seems to bond best either to a good cement backer board or to a cement-and-sand-based mud job in wet areas such as the shower and tub. Limestone also bonds well to drywall in areas where water isn't a concern. I did a mud job on the shower floor and used backer board for the shower walls and for the tub deck running up the walls a foot or so. For the rest of the wall work, I installed the limestone over the mildew-resistant drywall on the walls after priming the drywall with a skim coat of thinset the day before installing the tiles.

One often-overlooked characteristic of limestone is its translucence. Regular gray thinset has a tendency to darken the light-colored limestone, so I always install the tile with white latex-modified thinset. For this job I used Laticrete 253, a polymer-modified thinset mortar that mixes with water.

I spread the mortar for these limestone tiles with a ⅜-in. notched spreading trowel. Before installing each tile, I buttered the

Cutting and Installing Limestone

A wet saw is the best tool for cutting limestone, but installation is similar to regular tile.

Wet-saw jig from a tile scrap. A discarded tile cut at a 45° angle and clamped to the wet saw's sliding table streamlines cutting tiles for a diagonal layout.

Buttered back for better adhesion. Because of limestone's porous nature, the back of every tile receives a thin layer of mortar, a process known as buttering, which ensures sound attachment for each tile.

No special mortar for limestone. After the backs are buttered, the limestone tiles are set in the same latex-modified mortar used for many other types of tile. The lighter color was chosen because darker mortars can darken the limestone permanently.

back with a thin layer of thinset. This step may be slightly overkill, but it is cheap insurance for achieving a 100 percent bond when the tile is set in place.

Limestone Can Be Shaped with a Grinder and Sandpaper

When I'm installing an outside corner with ceramic tile, I have to order special tiles to achieve the bullnose edge. With stone tiles such as marble and limestone, edges can be carved or ground right into the edge of regular tiles. With polished marble, that edge has to be polished with a series of abrasive disks that get progressively finer. However, with limestone, once the bullnose edge is roughed out, I just go over it with 80-grit sandpaper to fine-tune the shape and then 120-grit sandpaper to smooth the finish. If I go any finer with the sandpaper, I have to be careful not to make the edge more polished than the tile itself.

One challenge in tile work made easy with limestone is forming tiles for an arched opening like the one I did over the shower entry in this bathroom. The first step was scribing the arched opening onto plywood for a template. Then I set a compass at 4 in. and paralleled my scribe line to form the arch. After cutting out the arch template, I traced the shape onto three pieces of limestone (see "Shaping Limestone" on p. 122).

It was easy to follow the outside radius of the arch with the wet saw, but the inside radius was challenging. I sawed over to the inside-radius line and removed the bulk of the waste. I then used my grinder to cut to the line.

The top of the radius still had to be bullnosed. The best way to put an even edge on a series of tiles is to join them together in the same order as they will be installed. For a square edge such as an outside corner of a wall, I just line up the tiles against a straightedge on the worktable and mold them as a single entity.

Shaping Limestone

Limestone can be worked almost like wood, taking shapes and finished edges with ease. But unlike highly polished marble, a light sanding is all limestone needs before it is ready to be installed.

Cut tiles are glued temporarily to the template. After the tiles are cut, the author glues them to the template. Having the tiles aligned the way they will be installed makes it easier to keep the edge shape consistent.

Arched door trim starts with a plywood template. After scribing the arch of the shower entry onto a piece of plywood and adding the top edge of the tile trim, that shape is transferred to the limestone.

A grinder roughs out the bullnose. An abrasive pad on an electric grinder fairs the curve of the arch and rounds over the tiles. A quick pass with 80-grit and then 120-grit sandpaper gets the tile ready for installation.

The arch, however, was a more formidable task. I began by gluing the pieces of limestone to the plywood template. I used a glue called Akemi™ (see "Sources" on p. 125), a quick-setting two-part polyester used to join stone to stone. In that capacity it forms a tenacious bond, but because I was gluing to plywood, I was able to break the bond and chip off the glue when I was finished shaping. Next, I used an electric grinder to round over the top edge of the arch to form half of a bullnose. After I finished the edge with sandpaper, the tiles were installed with the preshaped edge forming a continuous curve (see the photo at right).

Seal Twice, Grout Once

Cleaning and sealing the limestone before grouting are musts. At this stage, limestone should be sealed with a coat of an impregnator sealer to protect it from staining and to act as a grout release before grouting (see "Seal Limestone before and after Grouting" on p. 127). Manufacturers suggest testing the sealer on a small area of stone first. A good impregnator should not darken stone but rather leave stone in its natural state when it dries. I try to seal the edges of the tile as well so that the porous limestone doesn't suck the moisture out of the grout and cause it to cure prematurely.

I've used two different sealers, Miracle Sealants Porous Plus and StoneMasters Gold Seal (see "Sources"). I usually apply the sealer with a foam brush and then wipe down the tile with a clean rag. These sealers give off organic vapors, so if you're not installing the limestone in a well-ventilated area, I recommend wearing a respirator.

I grouted the limestone with a latex-modified floor grout made by TEC (see "Sources"). For these ⅛-in.-wide grout joints, I chose a sanded grout. Once the tile had been sealed and dried 24 hours, I grouted in pretty much the same way I do for most other tiles, raking the grout in diagonal

The arch goes up. Once the tiles are shaped and smoothed, they are installed on the wall, leaving the proper spacing for an attractive grout joint.

strokes across the grout joints to ensure that they get completely filled. When I'm grouting limestone, though, I try not to spread or cover more than 40 sq. ft. to 50 sq. ft. at a time. If any places in the grout joint did not get sealer, the grout could cure too quickly, making it difficult to work and also reducing its strength.

A Cleanup Before the Final Sealer

I waited two or three days to let the grout cure completely and then cleaned the tile thoroughly with a neutral-pH cleaner. Your local tile store can steer you toward several

A Mural in a Field of Stone

The crown jewel of this bathroom is a hand-painted ceramic-tile mural by Pat Wehrman of the Dodge Lane Potter Group in Sonora, Calif. (see "Sources" on p. 125). The mural—done in three sections—depicts a salt marsh with cattails and great blue herons, the same view someone is likely to have looking out the large bay window over the tub. Even though the individual pieces in each section were large, the mural went together like one of the jigsaw puzzles my sons love to play with.

I'm always extra careful handling the pieces of a mural. If a piece gets lost or broken, it is nearly impossible to replace it with one that will match the original both in size and in color.

Each section of the mural came with a map to help us reconstruct it accurately (see the top photo at right). First, James Mahony, my assistant, dry-fit all the sections together on a large sheet of plywood, while I put layout lines on the wall.

Next, I set the limestone tile on the wall up to where the mural began. Starting at the lower right-hand corner, I worked up and across each section of the mural. I set the mural tiles in the same white thinset I used for the limestone (see the photo on the facing page). Because of the irregular shapes and sizes of the mural pieces, I spread the thinset with the same ⅜-in. by ⅜-in. notched trowel. As each section was completed, I moved the pieces with my fingertips until the grout joints were perfect. A few strategically placed plastic wedges helped keep the pieces from drifting back.

The final installation step was adding the limestone frame around each section. The limestone was sealed, grouted and sealed again. Magically, as the limestone around the mural dried, the subtle colors in the stone enhanced and magnified all the hues in the hand-painted glaze of the mural.

Sources

Axson North America Inc.
800-365-8191
Akemi glue
www.axson-an.com

Dodge Lane Potter Group
Tiles@dlpg.com
Pat Wehrman
www.dlpg.com

Laticrete International Inc.
800-243-4788
Laticrete 253,
a polymer-modified thinset
www.laticrete.com

Miracle Sealants Company
800-350-1901
Porous Plus
www.miraclesealants.com

TEC
800-TEC-9002
TEC silicone sealer
www.tecspecialty.com

StoneMasters
800-851-2027
Gold Seal

Assembling a ceramic jigsaw puzzle. With the help of a paper map provided by the artist, the installer lays out the ceramic-tile mural carefully on a sheet of plywood (see the top photo on the facing page). After it is laid out, the mural is assembled from its lower corner; the installer works up and over until each section is completed (see the bottom photo on the facing page). When all the sections are set in place and framed with limestone, a final rinse and wipe down removes excess mortar from the hand-painted ceramic surface (see the photo above).

Waterproofing Membrane for a Built-In Shower Niche

A lot of the showers that we tile these days call for a tiled alcove or niche for shampoo bottles and soap. Most often, we line the framed opening with backer board and install the tile right on top. However, if I know that there is the possibility of a lot of water pressure hitting the niche directly, I line the backer board with a waterproof membrane. We decided to go that route with the niches in this shower.

The system we used here is made by Laticrete. After taping and sealing the backer board corners and seams inside the niche with thinset mortar, my assistant, James Mahony, began the membrane by applying a coat of Laticrete 9235 waterproofing liquid (see "Sources"), a black self-curing latex-rubber compound, over the whole interior of the niche. He took care not to get any black on the finished limestone walls of the shower. The compound is pretty noxious, so Mahony wore rubber gloves and a respirator while installing the membrane, especially in the confines of the shower stall.

Next, a nonwoven polyester fabric supplied with the kit was pressed into the wet compound (see the top photo at right). Mahony trimmed the excess out of the corners and then applied another coat of the black compound, thoroughly saturating the fabric (see the center photo at right). The compound combines with the fabric to create the waterproof membrane. The next day, Mahony came back and installed the limestone in the niche using a latex-modified thinset, also made by Laticrete, as an adhesive (see the bottom photo at right). Even with the waterproof membrane, we pitched the bottom of the niche slightly so that water would run out easily.

Fabric is pressed into the wet liquid. After the inside of the shampoo niche is coated with a latex-rubber liquid, a nonwoven polyester fabric is pressed into the liquid.

A second coat of latex-rubber saturates the fabric. When the fabric has been installed, a topcoat of rubber-latex liquid is applied to impregnate the fabric thoroughly.

Tiling the niche. After allowing the membrane to cure overnight, the limestone tile is then set into the same latex-modified thinset used in the rest of the room.

Seal Limestone before and after Grouting

A coat of sealer before grouting helps prevent the porous limestone from sucking moisture out of the grout as it cures. The final coat protects the tile from bathroom moisture.

The first coat of sealer. Sealing before the grout is spread keeps the tiles from absorbing the liquid in the grout and keeps the grout from staining the tiles.

The final coat of sealer. When all the tile is installed and grouted, a second coat of sealer is applied over the entire tiled surface. Sealer keeps the limestone from staining.

Protecting limestone from dark grouts. Here, the light-colored limestone has been masked off while black grout is applied to the marble border.

different cleaners. I then let the tile dry for a week or more, depending on the humidity, before applying the final coat of sealer. Some sealer manufacturers recommend that you wait 30 days before sealing to make sure all the moisture is released from the stone. Unlike other sealers, an impregnator sealer allows the tile to breathe and to release its vapors after the sealer is applied.

The French limestone in this bathroom is highly porous, so I doubled the final coat of sealer on the floor and tripled it on the tub deck and in the shower. When sealing shower walls, I start at the bottom and work my

The black grout that I used on the marble border can seriously stain the limestone. So after the limestone is sealed, I mask it off before spreading the black grout.

Should you discover scratches or marks that won't disappear with regular cleaning, those areas can be hit lightly with 120-grit or 220-grit sandpaper. Once I have sanded a tile to remove a mark, I then reapply a coat of sealer.

Tom Meehan is a second-generation tile installer, owner of Cape Cod Tileworks in Harwich, Massachusetts, and co-author of Build Like a Pro® Working with Tile *(The Taunton Press, Inc., 2005).*

Replacing a Broken Tile

■ BY JANE AEON

1. Isolate the victim. To keep the neighboring tiles intact, the first step is to score the grout lines with a utility knife. A few light passes do the trick.

It was bound to happen. The new floors have been finished for less than a week, and someone already has dropped a hammer on the kitchen's tile floor. Unless the tile guy is still on the job, you're either going to wait a long time or fix it yourself.

Luckily, it's a fairly easy fix, as long as you use the right technique. Although you can use a hammer and an old chisel to break out the damaged tile, this technique can be risky. Within grout joints tighter than $\frac{3}{16}$ in., hammer blows can chip or crack adjacent tiles. Hammering also can pulverize the substrate beneath the damaged tile.

Occasionally, I use a hole saw to cut out the center portion of a cracked tile. This technique is good for removing soft-bodied tile. It's usually a slow process, but I'm left with a hole in the tile that makes it easy to pry with the tip of a chisel or a screwdriver.

My preferred technique, however, is to use an angle grinder outfitted with a 4-in. diamond blade made by Pearl Abrasive (see

2. Protection is prevention. Before cutting, it's a good idea to mask off any nearby cabinets or furniture with plastic and tape. On the floor, angle brackets taped to the surrounding tiles protect them from inadvertent slips of the grinder's blade.

3. Diagonal cuts open up the tile. With both hands firmly holding the grinder, the author carefully plunges the blade into the tile's center and cuts diagonally, then along the tile's sides. A helper holds the vacuum hose to catch the dusty exhaust.

4. A junky tool still has its uses. Using a hammer and an old chisel or putty knife, the author works from the outside toward the tile's center, carefully prying out the pieces.

"Sources" on the facing page) and a shop vacuum. This technique is good for thick, soft-bodied tiles such as saltillo, but it works on others as well. The tile must be larger than 4 in., or there won't be room for a 4-in. grinder blade.

Basically, the trick is first to isolate the tile from neighboring tiles by removing the surrounding grout line, then carefully break the tile into pieces and remove it. Using a grinder can be messy unless you keep a vacuum nozzle trained on the dust stream. I mask off any surrounding cabinet faces or furniture, and also protect neighboring tiles with sheet metal or plywood in case I overcut. I mask off myself as well, by donning safety glasses, a dust mask and my hearing protection.

5. Make a clear space. After the tile is removed, all old thin-set and grout are scraped from the substrate, which is then vacuumed clean.

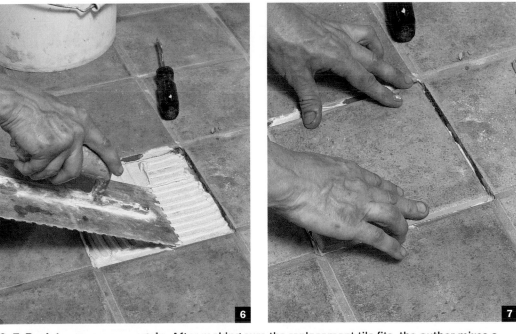

6, 7. Back to square one, again. After making sure the replacement tile fits, the author mixes a small batch of thinset, trowels it into the space (left), and sets the tile. After the thinset dries, the tile can be grouted.

Sources

Pearl Abrasive
800-969-5561
www.pearlabrasive.com

Makita
800-462-5482
www.makita.com

Dremel
800-437-3635
www.dremel.com

I start by making diagonal cuts, then make separate cuts that run parallel to the edges. The parallel cuts along the tile edges make it possible to position a chisel from the edge of a tile facing in so that the neighboring tile is not damaged. This technique is good for removing tiles with tight joints, like marble. There's also a cordless 3⅜-in. saw made by Makita with a slightly smaller diamond blade that comes in handy; I also use a Dremel tool fitted with a small #7134 diamond-point bit in the corners where the grinder can't reach (see "Sources").

Once the tile is removed, I scrape out any remaining thinset and vacuum the substrate. With fresh thinset and a new tile, the job is finished, except for the grouting work.

Jane Aeon is a tile contractor in Berkeley, California.

Installing an Electric Radiant Floor

■ BY TOM MEEHAN

Radiant System Installation

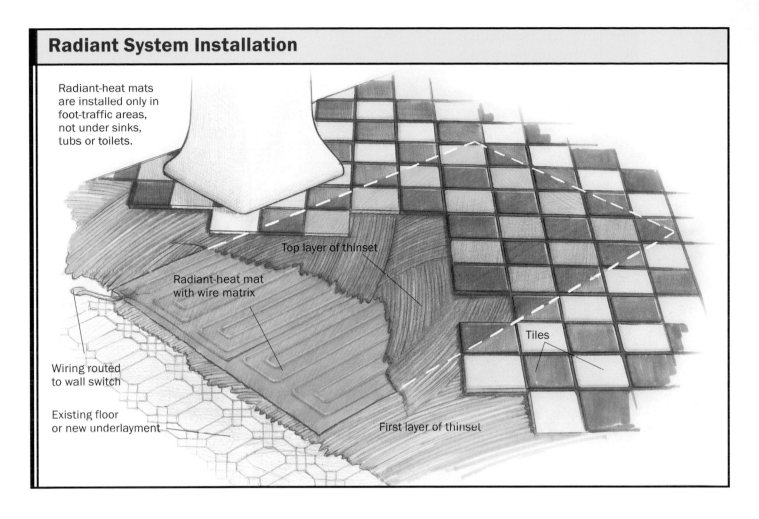

Radiant-heat mats are installed only in foot-traffic areas, not under sinks, tubs or toilets.

Top layer of thinset

Radiant-heat mat with wire matrix

Wiring routed to wall switch

Existing floor or new underlayment

Tiles

First layer of thinset

In my 30-plus years as a tile installer, I think the greatest improvement to tile floors is electric radiant heat. That warm feeling under your feet is something you will never take for granted, and it doesn't take much energy to operate an electric radiant floor. It can be as little as the energy it takes to run a 100-watt bulb. (Keep in mind that this is a comfort system, not the primary heat source for a room.)

Several types of electric radiant heat are on the market (see "Sources" on p. 136). Each electric radiant system has advantages, but they all have one thing in common: Like an electric blanket, they use a matrix of wires to conduct heat. For the remodeling project shown here, I used a NuHeat Mat (see "Sources"). This system consists of a mat made of a woven polyester fabric in which heat wires are embedded (see the drawing above). The mat is laminated to the subfloor with a layer of thinset, a special type of mortar that is used to adhere tile in areas that are exposed to moisture.

Heat Only the Areas That Are Walked On

First, determine how big a mat you need. If it's an open floor plan, measure the rectangular or square area that needs to be heated for an easy, off-the-shelf purchase. For complex installations, a detailed drawing submitted with a special order should include the location for the electrical hookup and the thermostatic controls. The manufacturer will configure a custom-fit system for your room. But remember that custom mats cost more than off-the-shelf ones and that you really need the wires only in the locations

The Benefits of an Electric Radiant-Heat Mat

- Comes in numerous standard sizes
- Inexpensive to operate
- Heats only the area you want heated
- Custom mats are available
- Can be installed over most existing floors
- Thin enough so that it won't adversely affect floor height

where you're likely to stand. In either case, heat wires should never run under a cabinet or toilet, where the wires can overheat and possibly burn out.

Electric Radiant Heat Can Go over Existing Materials

The remodeling job illustrated here takes a different kind of preparation than new construction. A few years ago, I would have ripped out the old floor, right down to the subfloor. Now, I save the mess and extra cost, and install over a properly prepared vinyl floor.

The work starts with the electrician drilling a hole for the wires in an inconspicuous spot that doesn't see much traffic (photo 1) or making a hole in the wall where the baseboard will cover it. Next, I

Locate the electrical feed. With the heat mat temporarily in place, the electrician drills in an inconspicuous spot to run wiring for the electrical feed and thermostatic control.

Don't rip it up, rough it up. The vinyl floor is roughed up so that the thinset will bond to it. The vinyl also serves as a slip sheet to prevent plywood seams from telegraphing through to the tile.

scarify the vinyl with a grinder or sander to give the thinset a surface it can bond to (photo 2). Then I nail off the floor with galvanized roofing nails 8 in. apart as if it were a piece of underlayment. This step ensures that no voids or inherent weak spots are in the floor. After nailing it off, I know this floor isn't going anywhere.

Installing the Heat Mat Is Not Difficult

Before I spread any thinset, I roll out the mat to make sure it fits. Knowing that the mat is working properly, I begin spreading a high-performance latex-modified thinset with a ¼-in. notched trowel (photo 3). A high-performance thinset means it can adhere to more resilient surfaces like vinyl because it has more polymers than other thinsets. Once the floor is coated, I can unroll the mat into the thinset (photo 4).

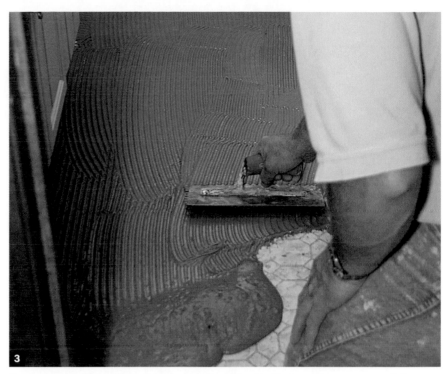

Use a ¼-in. notched trowel to spread the thinset. It's important to spread the thinset in one direction to allow the mat to sit evenly. Then unroll the mat at the door, pressing it into the thinset. Be careful not to work yourself into a corner while troweling thinset.

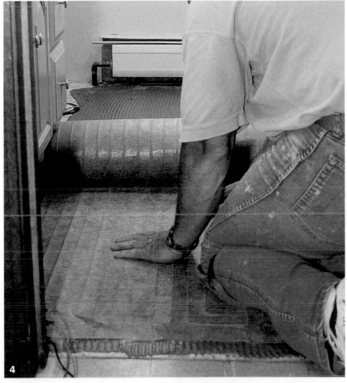

Unroll the mat, pushing it tight to keep it flat. Work the mat into the thinset, pressing it in while working forward. The wires in the mat are fragile, which is why setting it by hand is a good idea. The cabinets and fixtures are in place, making this installation easier.

Start from the middle and work your way out. To remove the voids or air pockets, a clean wood float does the trick. Be careful not to force the mat into place and possibly damage a connection.

Sources

EasyHeat®
800-537-4732
www.easyheat.com

Infloor® Radiant Heating Inc.
800-588-4470
www.infloor.com

NuHeat
800-778-9276
www.nuheat.com

STEP Warmfloor™
877-783-7832
www.warmfloor.com

SunTouch
888-432-8932
www.suntouch.net

WarmlyYours
800-875-5285
www.warmlyyours.com

6

Placing the sensor wire properly is critical. Once the mat is set, the electrician places the sensor wire. He will use strips of duct tape to hold it in place. It's important that the sensor wire doesn't cross the heating wires; otherwise, the thermostat won't get a proper reading.

7

Now it's a regular tile job. The thinset is troweled on with a ⅜-in. notched trowel with the trowel lines going in one direction. Take extra care when spreading thinset over the sensor wire. Once the tile is down, you might want to test the system. But wait a week for the thinset to cure before turning on the heat.

Before and after installation, I connect the mat to a typical multimeter, which can be bought at Sears for about $30*, to check for any damage to the wires. SunTouch® (see "Sources"), another electric-radiant-mat manufacturer, has a terrific proprietary alarm system called the Loud Mouth. If a wire is damaged during installation, the alarm sounds, and I know exactly where the problem is. Then I can have an electrician troubleshoot and repair any damage.

I work the mat forward, pushing it into the thinset. The wires are fragile and must be treated carefully. After the mat is spread out, I use a clean wood float to push it tight while getting rid of any voids or air pockets (see photo 5 on p. 135). I start from the middle of the mat and work my way out.

When the mat is set, the electrician lays the thermostat sensor between the heat wires (see photo 6). The sensor can't cross any heating wires, or it won't accurately record floor temperature. Next, he feeds the wires down the hole he drilled earlier and completes the connections.

Protect the Mat When Setting the Tile

My main concern now is protecting the heat mat from being damaged as I install the tile. By simply placing heavy cardboard wherever I work or step, I'm able to place the tile safely. I begin with a skim coat of thinset using the flat side of a trowel to permeate the fabric of the heat mat (photo 7). Then I apply more thinset and spread it with a ⅜-in. notched trowel. From this point, it becomes a typical tile installation.

Price estimates noted are from 2003.

Tom Meehan is a second-generation tile installer, owner of Cape Cod Tileworks in Harwich, Massachusetts, and co-author of Build Like a Pro® Working with Tile *(The Taunton Press, Inc., 2005).*

CREDITS

The articles in this book appeared in the following issues of *Fine Homebuilding*.

p. 4: Upgrading to a Tile Shower by Tom Meehan, issue 160. Photos by Roe A. Osborn, courtesy of *Fine Homebuilding*, © The Taunton Press, Inc., except photo on p. 5 by Charles Bickford, courtesy of *Fine Homebuilding*, © The Taunton Press, Inc.; photos of shower pans on p. 9 (top) Courtesy of Bonsal™ American (center & bottom) Courtesy of Lasco Bathware. Drawing by Dan Thornton, courtesy of *Fine Homebuilding*, © The Taunton Press, Inc.

p. 12: Tiling a Tub Surround by Michael Byrne, issue 92. Photos by Kevin Ireton, courtesy of *Fine Homebuilding*, © The Taunton Press, Inc.

p. 22: Tiling a Shower with Marble by Tom Meehan, issue 98. Photos by Jefferson Kolle, courtesy of *Fine Homebuilding*, © The Taunton Press, Inc.

p. 30: Tiling a Bathroom Floor by Dennis Hournay, issue 124. Photos by Scott Gibson, courtesy of *Fine Homebuilding*, © The Taunton Press, Inc. Drawing by Dan Thornton, courtesy of *Fine Homebuilding*, © The Taunton Press, Inc.

p. 40: Installing a Leakproof Shower Pan by Tom Meehan, issue 141. Photos by Roe A. Osborn, courtesy of *Fine Homebuilding*, © The Taunton Press, Inc. Drawing by Rick Daskam, courtesy of *Fine Homebuilding*, © The Taunton Press, Inc.

p. 48: Details from Great Bathrooms, issue 123. Photo on p. 48 by Kevin Ireton, courtesy of *Fine Homebuilding*, © The Taunton Press, Inc.; photo on p. 49 (left) © davidduncanlivingston.com; (top) by Charles Miller, courtesy of *Fine Homebuilding*, © The Taunton Press, Inc.; (bottom) © Carolyn L. Bates/carolynbates.com; Photos on p. 50 (left & top right) by Charles Miller, courtesy of *Fine Homebuilding*, © The Taunton Press, Inc.; (bottom right) by Chris Eden; Photo on p. 51 (top) © Grey Crawford; (bottom) © Tim Street-Porter.

p. 52: Putting Tile to Work in the Kitchen by Lane Meehan, issue 127. Photos by Roe A. Osborn, except photo on p. 53 by Andrea Rugg and photo on p. 54 by Judi Rutz, all courtesy of *Fine Homebuilding*, © The Taunton Press, Inc. Drawings by Paul Perreault, courtesy of *Fine Homebuilding*, © The Taunton Press, Inc.

p. 60: Tiling a Kitchen Counter by Dennis Hourany, issue 120. Photos by Scott Gibson, courtesy of *Fine Homebuilding*, © The Taunton Press, Inc. Drawings by Dan Thornton, courtesy of *Fine Homebuilding*, © The Taunton Press, Inc.

p. 71: Tiling over a Laminate Counter by David Hart, issue 130. Photos by Charles Bickford, courtesy of *Fine Homebuilding*, © The Taunton Press, Inc.

p. 76: Tiling a Backsplash by Tom Meehan, issue 167. Photos by Lindsay Meehan, courtesy of *Fine Homebuilding*, © The Taunton Press, Inc.

p. 82: Cutting Ceramic Tile by David Hart, issue 148. Photos by Charles Bickford, courtesy of *Fine Homebuilding*, © The Taunton Press, Inc.

p. 90: Grouting Tile by David Hart, issue 138. Photos by Charles Bickford, courtesy of *Fine Homebuilding*, © The Taunton Press, Inc. Drawings by Rick Daskam, courtesy of *Fine Homebuilding*, © The Taunton Press, Inc.

p. 98: A Different Approach to Tiling Floors by Tom Meehan, issue 106. Photos by Roe A. Osborn, courtesy of *Fine Homebuilding*, © The Taunton Press, Inc.

p. 106: Glass Tile by Tom Meehan, issue 161. Photos by Charles Bickford, except photos on pp. 112–113 by Dan Thornton, all courtesy of *Fine Homebuilding*, © The Taunton Press, Inc.

p. 114: Decorating Tile at Home by Nancy Selvin, issue 78. Photos by Steve Selvin, courtesy of *Fine Homebuilding*, © The Taunton Press, Inc.

p. 118: Tiling with Limestone by Tom Meehan, issue 118. Photos by Roe A. Osborn, courtesy of *Fine Homebuilding*, © The Taunton Press, Inc.

p. 128: Replacing a Broken Tile by Jane Aeon, issue 168. Photos by Charles Bickford, courtesy of *Fine Homebuilding*, © The Taunton Press, Inc.

p. 132: Installing an Electric Radiant Floor by Tom Meehan, issue 159. Photos by Roe A. Osborn, except photo on p. 132 by Kevin Ireton, and photos on p. 134 (top & bottom left) by Scott Phillips, all courtesy of *Fine Homebuilding*, © The Taunton Press, Inc. Drawing by Bob LaPointe, courtesy of *Fine Homebuilding*, © The Taunton Press, Inc.

INDEX

Taunton's FOR PROS BY PROS Series
A collection of the best articles from *Fine Homebuilding* magazine.

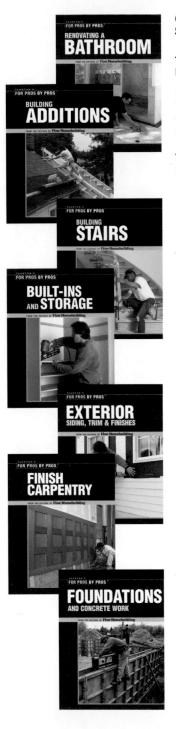

Other Books in the Series:

Taunton's For Pros By Pros:
RENOVATING A BATHROOM

ISBN 1-56158-584-X
Product #070702
$17.95 U.S.
$25.95 Canada

Taunton's For Pros By Pros:
BUILDING ADDITIONS

ISBN 1-56158-699-4
Product #070779
$17.95 U.S.
$25.95 Canada

Taunton's For Pros By Pros:
BUILDING STAIRS

ISBN 1-56158-653-6
Product #070742
$17.95 U.S.
$25.95 Canada

Taunton's For Pros By Pros:
BUILT-INS AND STORAGE

ISBN 1-56158-700-1
Product #070780
$17.95 U.S.
$25.95 Canada

Taunton's For Pros By Pros:
EXTERIOR SIDING, TRIM & FINISHES

ISBN 1-56158-652-8
Product #070741
$17.95 U.S.
$25.95 Canada

Taunton's For Pros By Pros:
FINISH CARPENTRY

ISBN 1-56158-536-X
Product #070633
$17.95 U.S.
$25.95 Canada

Taunton's For Pros By Pros:
FOUNDATIONS AND CONCRETE WORK

ISBN 1-56158-537-8
Product #070635
$17.95 U.S.
$25.95 Canada

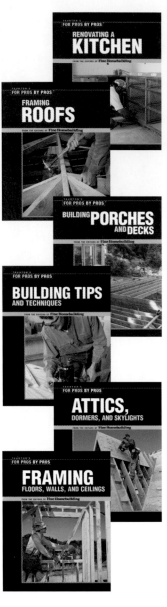

Taunton's For Pros By Pros:
RENOVATING A KITCHEN

ISBN 1-56158-540-8
Product #070637
$17.95 U.S.
$25.95 Canada

Taunton's For Pros By Pros:
FRAMING ROOFS

ISBN 1-56158-538-6
Product #070634
$17.95 U.S.
$25.95 Canada

Taunton's For Pros By Pros:
BUILDING PORCHES AND DECKS

ISBN 1-56158-539-4
Product #070636
$17.95 U.S.
$25.95 Canada

Taunton's For Pros By Pros:
BUILDING TIPS AND TECHNIQUES

ISBN 1-56158-687-0
Product #070766
$17.95 U.S.
$25.95 Canada

Taunton's For Pros By Pros:
ATTICS, DORMERS, AND SKYLIGHTS

ISBN 1-56158-779-6
Product #070834
$17.95 U.S.
$25.95 Canada

Taunton's For Pros By Pros:
FRAMING FLOORS, WALLS, AND CEILINGS

ISBN 1-56158-758-3
Product #070821
$17.95 U.S.
$25.95 Canada

For more information visit our website at www.taunton.com.